LA GRANGE PUBLIC LIBRARY
3 1320 00355 4149

P9-BZQ-766

WITHDRAWN
WD
La Grange Public Library
La Grange, Illinois

BOOKS

Go little booke, to suttle world,
And shew thy simple face,
And forward pass, and do not turne,
Nor slacken in thy pace:
Desire those men that like thee not,
To lay thee down againe,
Till some sweet nappe and harmless sleepe,
Hath settled troubled brayne.

— Anonymous

"Still Life" by Francois Bonvin, 1876. (The National Gallery, London.)

Front Cover: *A woodcut depicting Dr. Johnson and his bookseller in a heated discussion over a book.*
— *Sir Lionel Lindsay (1922).*

VAN NOSTRAND REINHOLD COMPANY
NEW YORK CINCINNATI TORONTO LONDON MELBOURNE

Library of Congress Catalog Card Number 81-2465
ISBN 0-442-21901-6

Printed in the United States of America

Design/Maher & Murtagh

Published by Van Nostrand Reinhold Company
135 West 50th Street, New York, NY 10020

Van Nostrand Reinhold Limited
1410 Birchmount Road
Scarborough, Ontario M1P 2E7, Canada

Van Nostrand Reinhold Australia Pty. Ltd.
17 Queen Street
Mitcham, Victoria 3132, Australia

Van Nostrand Reinhold Company Limited
Molly Millars Lane
Wokingham, Berkshire, England

16 15 14 13 12 11 10 9 8 7 6 5 4 3 2 1

Library of Congress Cataloging in Publication Data

Donaldson, Gerald.
Books.
1. Books and reading.
II. Title.
Z1003.D68 028'.9 81-2465
ISBN 0-442-21901-6 AACR2

For Elizabeth

Acknowledgments

The sources of quoted text are given after each relevant passage. Where required, illustration sources are noted in the captions. All books from which textual or illustrative material have been taken, as well as books for further reference, are listed in the Bibliography. The author has taken all possible care to trace the ownership of every work reproduced in this book and to make full acknowledgment for its use. If any errors have accidentally occurred, they will be corrected in subsequent editions, provided notification is sent to the publisher.

ILLUSTRATION CREDITS
Certain abbreviations have been made as follows:

ALS	*Anecdotes Literary and Scientific*
BA	The Bettmann Archive, New York
BBC	BBC Hulton Picture Library, London
BD	*The Book of Days*
B-H	*The Book-Hunter in London*
BL	Reproduced by permission of the British Library, London
The Book	*The Book* by Henri Bouchet
CFGOB	*Comfort Found in Good Old Books*
EAA	*Early Advertising Art*
Mansell	The Mansell Collection, London
ME	Mary Evans Picture Library, London
MTL	The Metropolitan Toronto Library
NG	Reproduced by courtesy of the Trustees, The National Gallery, London
PP	*The Pentateuch of Printing*
PRF	*The Picture Reference File*
SB	*The Story of the Bookplate*
TB	*A Treasury of Bookplates*
TG	The Tate Gallery, London
V&A	Victoria and Albert Museum, London, Crown Copyright

Illustrations are credited from left to right and from top to bottom.
Front Cover: Woodcut by Sir Lionel Lindsay, courtesy of Peter Lindsay, Kirribilli, Australia.
Page 1: MTL. 2: NG. 4: *SB*. 6–7: BL Additional MS 42131 f.73.
8: *The Book.* 10: BL Additional MS 18850 f.24.
11: *The Book,* Mansell. 12: *PP, PRF.*
13: BBC. 14: BL Harley MS 2897 f.186V.
15: BL Additional MS 39810 f.7. 16: *BD.*
17: *BD.* 18: *The Book.* 19: BA.
20: *EEA, CFGOB, EAA.* 21: *The Book, The Book* by D.C. McMurtrie.
22: *The Book, A History of Printing.* 23: NG.
24: *EAA* (two). 25: *London Illustrated News, United States Magazine.*
26: NG. 28: MTL.
29: *PRF.* 30: Mansell, *PRF,* V&A. 31: Mansell, *PRF.*
32: *PRF.* 33: *PRF, ALS* (two). 34: BBC.
35: *EAA.* 36: *BD.*
37: *PRF.* 38: *PRF.* 39: *CFGOB, B-H.*
40: *SB.* 42: *BD* (two). 43: ME, Mansell.
44: *The Bookworm.* 46: *B-H* (two), *PRF.*
47: *The Book.* 48: *EAA.* 49: *PP.* 50: *B-H, BD.* 51: *BD.*
52: V&A. 54: *B-H, BD.* 55: *BD, ALS.* 56: *PRF.* 58: *PRF.*
59: *BD* (two). 60: *PRF* (two). 61: *The Tour of Dr. Syntax.* 62: MTL.
64: ME. 65: *B-H,* MTL.
66: Copyright Museo Del Prado, Madrid. 68: *BH.*
69: *TB.* 70: MTL. 71: *Micrographia.* 72: *The Book.*
73: *TB,* BBC. 74: Mansell. 75: *PRF.* 76: *PRF,* ME.
77: *SB.* 78–79: NG. 81: BA. 82: NG. 84: *PRF.*
85: *PRF, SB.* 86: V&A. 87: BL Harley MS 2897 f.340v.
88: *PRF, CFGOB.* 89: *ALS.* 90: *BD.* 91: NG. 92: TG.
93: *B-H.* 94: V&A. 96: *The Book.* 97: *TB,* BA. 98: BBC.
99: *PRF* (two). 100: *PRF.* 101: V&A. 102: *BD* (two).
103: *Curiosities of Literature.* 104: *PRF, TB.*
105: *B-H* (two). 106: *B-H, SB* (two). 107: *SB, PRF.*
108: *TB.* 110: *PP, PRF.* 111: *PRF.* 112: *PRF,* TG. 113: *TB* (two).
114: *B-H* (two).
115: *B-H, PRF.* 116: *PRF,* BBC. 117: *PRF* (three). 119: *PRF, SB.*
121: ME, *PRF.* 122: ME, *EAA.*
123: *SB.* 124–125: *EAA, PRF.*

Contents

An Illuminated Letter "B" from the Bedford Psalter and Hours, *1422. (The British Library, London.)*

The Papermaker

The Typefounder

The Printer

The Binder

Early Bookmaking, from an engraving by Jost Amman, 1568.

CHAPTER ONE

Bookmaking

The six-thousand-year-old history of books from the first primitive attempts to collect scribblings between covers to the fabulous illuminated manuscripts of medieval times and the proliferation of the printed word.

St. Mark writing his gospel, from the Bedford Hours, *1423. (The British Library, London.)*

Letters are symbols which turn matter into spirit.
— Alphonse de Lamartine, 1858

The Oldest Writing in the World?

Among the oldest writing in the world, on stone, wood, papyrus, or parchment, is probably a monument, with an inscription in Egyptian Hieroglyphics (preserved in the Ashmolean Museum at Oxford). It is the cornice over a false door of a tomb, the frame of the doorway being still in existence in the Boulak Museum at Cairo, while the only piece which bears an inscription was presented by Dr. Huntington to the University in 1683. On one side is a seated figure representing Shera, a priest of Send; on the other, another seated figure of a female. Between them is a table, and on it and below it offerings made to Send. This Send was a king of the second dynasty; and even if we allow his cult to have continued for 1000 years, the date of the stone would still have to be assigned to about 4000 B.C. The astonishing thing is, that even in this remote antiquity the inscription (the important part of which runs along the upper part) exhibits, not only ideographic writing or only syllabic, but actually alphabetical! The cartouche bearing the name of the king is written alphabetically thus:

$$\begin{matrix} N \\ \\ D \end{matrix} S = \text{Send.}$$

It adds to the interest of this venerable monument that Egyptian Hieroglyphics are in the direct line of the ancestry of our own alphabet.

— Falconer Madan, *Books in Manuscript*

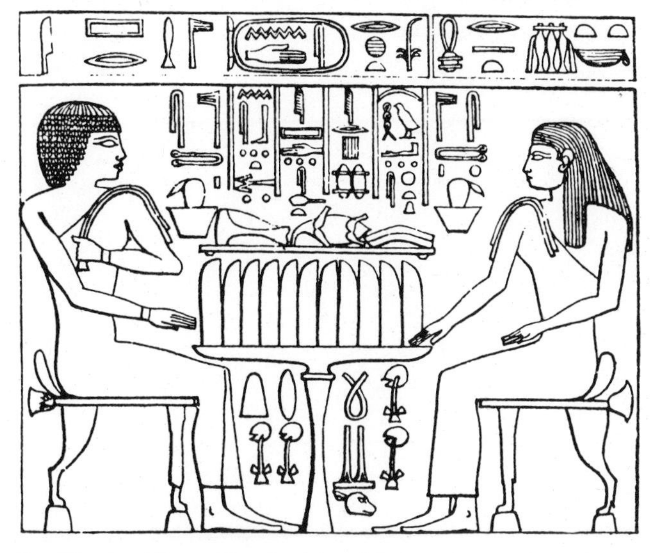

Possibly the oldest writing in the world.

EARLY ALPHABET'S FROM PHŒNICIAN TO ROMAN. F.L.V.

Modern Characters	Ancient Phœnician	Ancient Hebrew	Ancient Greek	Samaritan	Oscan & Samnite	Early Roman	Modern Hebrew	Greek Names
A	[illegible]	[illegible]	[illegible]	[illegible]	[illegible]	[illegible] A	א Aleph	Alpha
B	[illegible]	[illegible]	[illegible]	[illegible]	[illegible]	B B	ב Beth	Beta
G	[illegible]	[illegible]	[illegible]	[illegible]	[illegible]	C G	ג Gimel	Gamma
D	[illegible]	[illegible]	[illegible]	[illegible]	[illegible]	Δ D	ד Daleth	Delta
E	[illegible]	[illegible]	[illegible]	[illegible]	[illegible]	E	ה He	Epsilon
F	[illegible]	[illegible]	[illegible]	[illegible]	[illegible]	F	ו Vau	Digamma
Z	Z	—	[illegible]	[illegible]	[illegible]	[illegible]	ז Zain	Zeta
HE	[illegible]	E	[illegible] H	[illegible]	[illegible]	H	ח Cheth	Eta
TH	[illegible]	—	⊙	[illegible]	—	—	ט Teth	Theta
I	[illegible]	[illegible]	[illegible]	[illegible]	[illegible]	|	י Yod	Iota
K	[illegible]	[illegible]	[illegible] K	[illegible]	[illegible]	K	כ ך Caph	Kappa
L	[illegible]	L	[illegible]	[illegible]	[illegible]	L	ל Lamed	Lambda
M	[illegible]	[illegible]	[illegible]	[illegible]	[illegible]	M	מ ם Mem	Mem
N	[illegible]	[illegible]	[illegible] N	[illegible]	[illegible]	N	נ ן Nun	Nun
S	[illegible]	—	[illegible]	[illegible]	—	—	ס Samech	Xsi
O	[illegible]	[illegible]	O	[illegible]	[illegible]	[illegible]	ע Ain.	Omicron
P	[illegible]	[illegible]	[illegible]	[illegible]	[illegible]	[illegible]	פ ף Pe	Pi
TZ	[illegible]	[illegible]	Z	[illegible]	-	—	צ ץ Tsade	
KO	[illegible]	[illegible]	[illegible]	[illegible]	-	Q	ק Koph	Koph
R	[illegible]	[illegible]	[illegible] R	[illegible]	[illegible]	R	ר Resch	Resch
SH	[illegible]	[illegible]	[illegible]	[illegible]	[illegible]	S	ש Shin	Sigma
T	[illegible]	[illegible]	[illegible] T	[illegible]	T	T	ת Tau	Tau

The ancestry of our alphabet.

Without words, without writing and without books there would be no history, there could be no concept of humanity.
— Hermann Hesse (1877-1962)

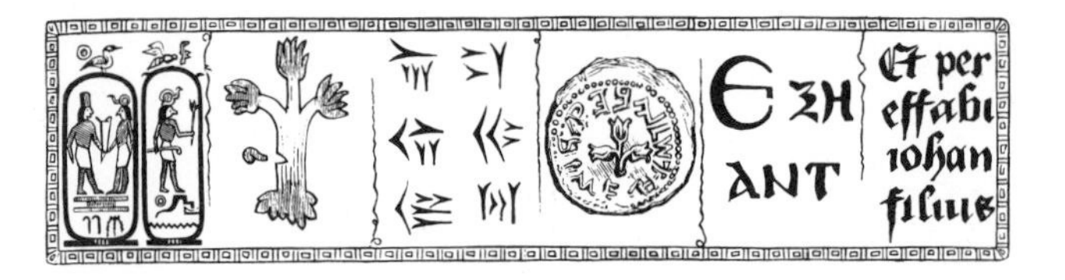

Early Writing Materials and the Origin of the Word 'Book'

The most ancient mode of writing was on bricks, tiles, and oyster-shells, and on tables of stone; afterwards on plates of various materials, on ivory, on barks of trees, on leaves of trees.

Engraving memorable events on hard substances was giving, as it were, speech to rocks and metals. In the book of Job mention is made of writing on stone, on rocks, and on sheets of lead. On tables of stone Moses received the law written by the finger of God. Hesiod's works were written on leaden tables: lead was used for writing, and rolled up like a cylinder, as Pliny states. They afterwards engraved on bronze: the laws of the Cretans were on bronze tables; the Romans etched their public records on brass.

Among these early inventions many were singularly rude, and miserable substitutes for a better material. In the shepherd state they wrote their songs with thorns and awls on straps of leather, which they wound round their crooks. The Icelanders appear to have scratched their *runes*, a kind of hieroglyphics, on walls; and, according to one of the Norse sagas, one northern hero appears to have had nothing better than his own chair and a bed to perpetuate his own heroic acts on. The ancient Arabs, according to the history of Mahomet, seem to have carved on the shoulder-bones of sheep remarkable events with a knife, and tying them with a string, hung up these sheep-bone chronicles.

The laws of the emperors were published on wooden tables, painted with ceruse. A thin paste of wax was also used on tables of wood, that it might more easily admit of erasure, for daily use.

They wrote with an iron bodkin, as they did on the other substances we have noticed. The stylus was made sharp at one end to write with, and blunt and broad at the other, to deface and correct easily. But the Romans forbad the use of this sharp instrument, from the circumstance of many persons having used them as daggers. A schoolmaster was killed by the Pugillares or table-books, and the styles of his own scholars. They substituted a stylus made of the bone of a bird, or other animal; so that their writings resembled engravings. When they wrote on softer materials, they employed reeds and canes split like our pens at the points.

In the progress of time the art of writing consisted in painting with different kinds of ink. This novel mode of writing occasioned them to invent other materials proper to receive their writing; the thin bark of certain trees and plants, or linen; and at length, when this was found apt to become mouldy, they prepared the skins of animals; on the dried skins of serpents, were once written the Iliad and Odyssey. The first place where they began to dress these skins was Pergamus, in Asia; whence the Latin name is derived of Pergamenae or parchment.

When the Egyptians employed for writing the bark of a plant or reed, called papyrus, or paper-rush, it superseded all former modes, for its convenience. Formerly it grew in great quantities on the sides of the Nile. After the eighth century the papyrus was superseded by parchment. The Chinese made their paper with silk. The use of paper is of great antiquity.

Before the use of parchment and paper passed to the Romans, they used the thin peel found between the wood and the bark of trees. This skinny substance they call *liber*, from whence the Latin word *liber*, a book, and library and librarian in the European languages, and the French *livre* for book; but we of northern origin derive our *book* from the Danish *bog*, the birch-tree, because that being the most plentiful in Denmark was used to engrave on.

— Isaac Disraeli, *Curiosities of Literature*

The Celebrated Library at Alexandria

The celebrated library at Alexandria was probably the largest collection ever brought together before the invention of printing. It is said to have been founded by Ptolemy Soter about 283 B.C., and increased by his successors until it contained, according to Aulus Gellius, 700,000 volumes. During the siege of Alexandria by Julius Caesar, a great part of this library was burnt by a fire, which spread from the shipping to the city; it was soon re-established and augmented by the addition of the library founded by Eumenes, King of Pergamus (the accredited inventor of parchment), which collection, amounting to 200,000 volumes, Marc Antony presented to Cleopatra. Alexandria flourished as one of the chief seats of literature until it was taken by the Arabs, 640 A.D. The library was then burnt, according to the story generally believed, in consequence of the fanatic decision of the Caliph Omar: 'If these writings of the Greeks agree with the Book of God, they are useless and need not be preserved; if they disagree, they are pernicious, and ought to be destroyed.' Accordingly, it is said, they were employed to heat the 4000 baths of the city; and such was their number that six months were barely sufficient for the consumption of the precious fuel.

— John Power, *A Handy-Book About Books*

For several days after my first book was published I carried it about in my pocket, and took surreptitious peeps at it to make sure that the ink had not faded.

— James Matthew Barrie (1860-1937)

Early Bookmaking

It is supposed that the square form of book began to prevail in Rome in imitation of the tablets used for private memoranda, which were at first waxed plates of metal within a cover more or less richly decorated, and protected by raised edges. These tablets were afterwards displaced by leaves of vellum, sometimes of different colours, to the number of five or six. Such tablets, within richly carved ivory covers, were, during the period of the Eastern empire, presented to consuls or other high functionaries on their nomination to office. Eventually, it became customary for private persons to present each other with tablets, often with complimentary poems ready written on the leaves of vellum, the covers naturally becoming objects for decorative embellishment. Small books of poems were prepared for sale in the same way, as the old rolled form did not afford such scope for decoration as the pair of panels which enclosed and protected the tablets. This form of book probably arose in the East shortly before the removal of the capital to Constantinople, as the name by which tablets of that kind were distinguished was the Greek term *diptych*. The period which may be assigned for the general adoption of the square form for books was probably not earlier than the fourth century.

— John Power, *A Handy-Book about Books*

"A Reading from Homer" by Alma Tadema.

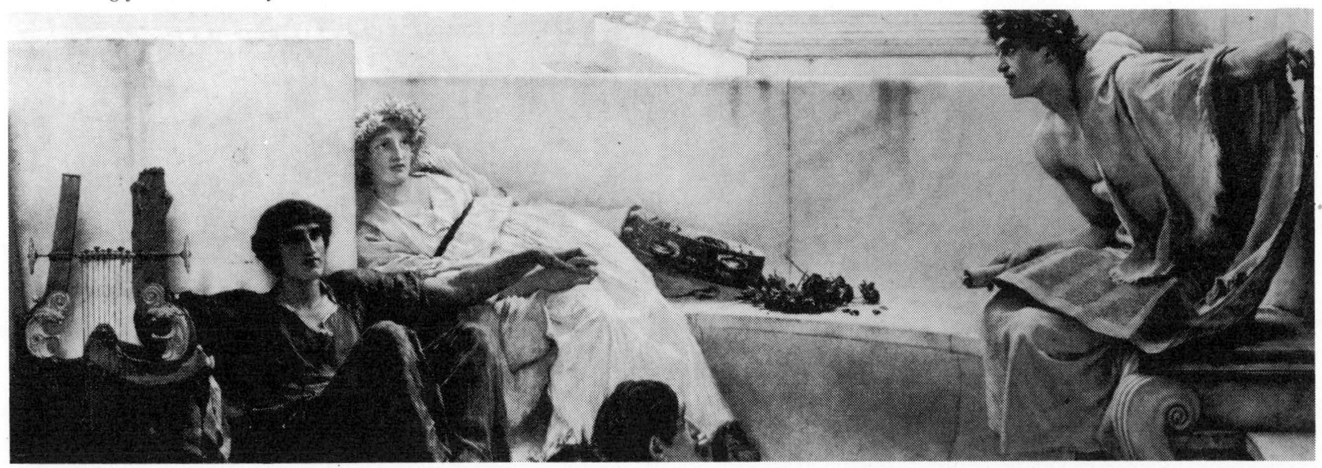

With one sole pen I wrote this book,
Made of a grey goose quill;
A pen it was when I it took,
And a pen I leave it still.
— Philemon Holland, from a book he wrote in 1610

Making a Medieval Manuscript

Let us now observe how a scribe would act at the beginning of his six-hour daily task. A section of plain parchment is brought to him to be written on, each sheet still separate from the others, though loosely put in the order and form in which it will be subsequently bound. First, when the style and general size of the intended writing has been fixed, which would be a matter of custom, the largest style being reserved for psalters and other books to be used for public services on a desk or lectern, the sheets have to be ruled. Down each side of the page, holes were pricked at proper intervals with an awl, and a hard, dry, metal stilus used to draw the lines from hole to hole, with others perpendicular to mark the margins; space was also left for illuminations when the place could be judged beforehand. The stilus made a furrow on one side of the parchment and raised a ridge on the other side, and was carried right across a sheet of parchment.

The scribe has now his ruled leaves before him, his pen and ink in readiness, and the volume to be copied on a desk beside him; he may begin to transcribe. How simple this seems! He is forbidden to correct, but just simply copy down letter for letter what is before him; no responsibility, except for power of reading and for accuracy, is laid on him.

When the copyist had finished a quaternion (four sheets folded in two), the writing was often compared with the original by another person (*diorthōtēs*; in Latin, corrector). Next, the sheets were given over to the rubricator, who inserted titles, sometimes concluding notes (called colophones), liturgical directions, lists of chapters, headlines, and the like; and finally, if need were, to the illuminator. Nothing then remained, but that the binder's art should sew together the sections, and put them in their covering.

— Falconer Madan, *Books in Manuscript*

St. Jude writing, from the Breviary of John, The Fearless, *1415. (The British Library, London.)*

To a 13th-Century Manuscript

Missal of the Gothic age,
Missal with the blazoned page,
Whence, O Missal, hither come,
From what dim Scriptorium?

Whose the name that wrought thee thus,
Ambrose or Theophilus,
Bending, through the waning light,
O'er thy vellum scraped and white;

Weaving 'twixt thy rubric lines
Sprays and leaves and quaint designs;
Setting round thy border scrolled
Buds of purple and of gold?

Ah! — a wondering brotherhood,
Doubtless, by that artist stood,
Raising o'er his careful ways
Little choruses of praise!

Glad when his deft hand would paint
Strife of Sathanas and Saint,
Or in secret coign entwist
Jest of cloister humourist.

Well the worker earned his wage
Bending o'er the blazoned page!
Tired the hand and tired the wit
Ere the final Explicit!

Not as ours the books of old —
Things that steam can stamp and fold;
Not as ours the books of yore —
Rows of type and nothing more.

Then a book was still a Booke,
Where a wistful man might look,
Finding something through the whole
Beating — like a human soul.

In that growth of day by day,
When to labour was to pray,
Surely something vital passed
To the patient page at last;

Something that one still perceives
Vaguely present in the leaves!
Something from the worker lent;
Something mute — but eloquent!

— Austin Dobson (1840–1921)

Books must be read as deliberately and reservedly as they were written.

— Henry David Thoreau (1817-1862)

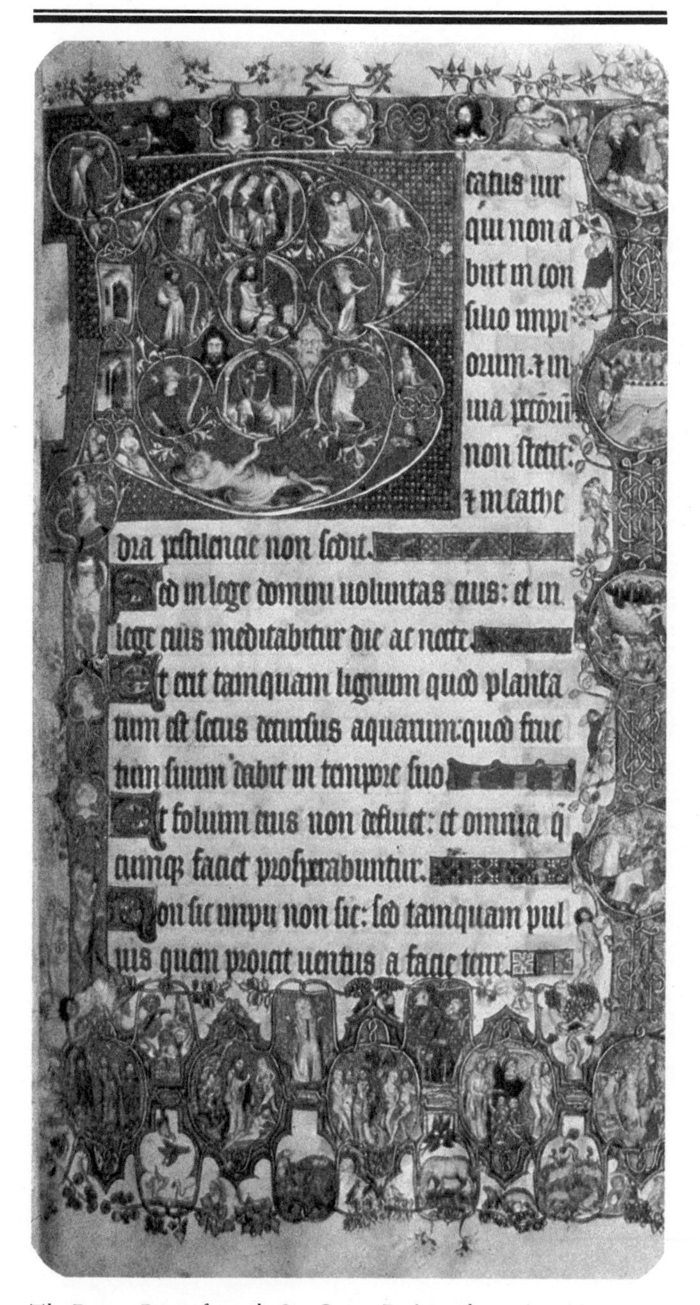

The Beatus Page, from the St. Omer Psalter, *begun in 1330. (The British Library, London.)*

'Tis the good reader that makes the good book.
— Ralph Waldo Emerson (1803-1882)

Books in Chains

Why chain books?

It is certainly a distressing as well as a suggestive sight to see books in chains. Distressing, because a good book is like a strong man, and when chained is as shorn Samson among the Philistines. No one nowadays would think of chaining books to desks or library shelves, for our ideas about such matters have indeed altered from those prevalent when such a custom obtained; so that the mere sight of a single survival of this rude practice is strongly suggestive, not only of advance in education and literary enlightenment, but also of the power of the printing press, through whose influence alone her offspring, as well as her parents, the manuscript books, have been redeemed from their chains.

Before the invention of Printing, books were scarce and dear, and it was the custom of the College authorities to lend single volumes to students for one year, to be then returned with evidence of their having been profitably studied. No doubt positive loss was one result, and injustice to non-favoured students another; but books borrowed have always been proverbial for not coming home to roost, and chaining seemed a natural way of securing them for general use. This appears to me more likely to have been the object of chaining than the prevention of theft.

The custom of fastening books to their shelves by chains was common at an early period throughout all Europe. When a book was given to a mediaeval library it was necessary, in the first place, to buy a chain, and, if the book was of especial value, a pair of clasps; secondly, to employ a smith to put them on; and, lastly, a painter to write the name and class-mark across the fore-edge. Large collections of chained books were for the use of particular bodies of students; but when religious zeal made many people feel the want of spiritual food, it led to the chaining of single volumes in churches, where any parishioner, able to read, could satisfy his soul. The Bible was, of course, one of the most common, and among others were Foxe's *Book of Martyrs*, the various works of Bishop Jewel, and other Divines.

— William Blades, *Books in Chains*

The Horn-Book

The Horn-book was a thin board of oak about nine inches long and five or six wide, on which were printed the alphabet, the nine digits, and sometimes the Lord's Prayer. It had a handle, and was covered in front with a sheet of thin horn to prevent its being soiled, and the back-board was ornamented with a rude sketch of St. George and the Dragon. The board and its horn cover were held together by a narrow frame of brass. Formerly the first "book" put in the hands of the school-boy.

A seventeenth century Horn-Book.

Thee will I sing in comely wainscot bound
And golden verge enclosing thee around;
The faithful horn before, from age to age
Preserving thy invulnerable page;
Behind, thy patron saint in armor shines,
With sword and lance to guard the sacred lines.
Th'instructive handle's at the bottom fixed,
Lest wrangling critics should pervert the text.

— Tickell, *The Horn-Book*

Their books of stature small they took in hand,
Which with pellucid horn secured are,
To save from finger wet the letter fair.

— Shenstone, *The School-Mistress*

— William S. Walsh, *A Handy-Book of Literary Curiosities*

A Stolen Bible

Fast bind, fast find: my Bible was well bound;
A Thiefe came fast, and loose my Bible found;
Was't bound and loose at once? how can that be?
'Twas loose for him, although 'twas bound for me.

— John Taylor, *Epigrammes*, 1651

A chained Bible in Cumnor Church, Leicestershire, England.

There are books of which the backs and covers are by far the best parts.
— Charles Dickens (1812-1870)

A Short History of Book Binding

An eleventh century French binding in gold ornamented with jewels.

The earliest germ of bookbinding was to be found among the Assyrians, who wrote their books on terra-cotta tablets, and enclosed these tablets in clay receptacles which had to be broken before the contents could be reached. Tamil manuscripts of extreme antiquity are also extant, to which a rounded form has been given by the simple expedient of using larger leaves at the centre and adding others gradually shortened at each side. The circle is surrounded by a metal band, tightly fastened by a hook. How far the Greeks improved upon these primitive methods it is difficult to say, as their literature furnishes no details on the subject, but there is a tradition that the Athenians raised a statue to Phillatius, who invented a glue for fastening together leaves of parchment or papyrus. The papyrus rolls of the Romans were in their way handsome specimens of the art of bookbinding, with their leather covers, gold bosses, gold cylinder, and perfumed illuminated leaves. Mediaeval bindings were generally of carved ivory, metal, or wood, covered with stamped leather, and frequently adorned with bosses of gold, gems, and precious stones. Of course they could not be kept on shelves, like modern volumes: they would have scratched one another. Each had its embroidered silken case, or *chemise*, and, when especially valuable, its casket of gold.

With the invention of printing, regular bookbinding, in the modern sense of the word, began. Wooden covers and stamped pig-skin gradually gave way before the lighter styles introduced by the Italians and perfected by the French. Early in the sixteenth century morocco was introduced, the arts of the printer and the binder were differentiated, and new decorations testified to the conservation of energy thus attained and its direction into the right channel. The bindings affected by the great people of the court of France had a distinct individuality. Henri II and Diane de Poictiers displayed the crescent, the bow, and the quiver of Diana, and the blended initials *H.* and *D.* Francis I had his salamanders, Marguerite the flower from which she derived her name. The pious Henri III rejoiced in figures of the Crucifixion, in counterfeit tears with long curly tails, and in various emblems of mortality. In the reign of Louix XIV it became fashionable to emboss the owner's arms upon his books.

In the eighteenth century, ornamental figures of birds and flowers became common, together with mosaics of various-colored leather. The French Revolution brought temporary ruin upon the art of bookbinding. Morocco was culpable luxury, and coats of arms were an insult to the Republic. There is an oft-quoted story of the French literary man of 1794, a great reader, who always stripped off the covers of his books and threw them out of his window. What had a citizen to do with morocco bindings, with the gildings of Le Cascon or Derome, the trappings of an effete aristocracy? Perhaps he was right. A working-man of letters, like a working-man of any other guild, cannot use a gorgeously-bound book as one of the implements of his trade. He puts an inky pen into the leaves of one volume, he lays another on its face, he uses the leg of a chair to keep a folio open and to mark the pregnant passage. But there is a class of drones, of literary voluptuaries and sybarites, who love to see their libraries well clothed.

Perhaps the most unique binding in the world is in the Albert Memorial Exhibition in Exeter, England. It is a Tegg's edition of Milton (1852), and, according to an affadivit pasted on the fly-leaf, the binding is part of the skin of one George Cudmore, who was executed at Devon March 25, 1830. The skin is dressed white, and looks something like pig-skin in grain and texture.

— William S. Walsh, *A Handy-Book of Literary Curiosities*

The peace of great books be for you,
Stains of pressed clover leaves on pages,
Bleach of the light of years held in leather.
— Carl Sandburg (1878-1967)

An Ale-sodden Bookbinder

In the eighteenth century, when the pursuit of book-collecting was almost approaching to the nature of a mania, a great want was felt of an artist capable of providing suitable habiliments for the treasures of literature — of constructing caskets worthy of the jewels which they enshrined. At this eventful crisis, as Dr. Dibdin informs us, "Roger Payne rose like a star, diffusing lustre on all sides, and rejoicing the hearts of all true sons of bibliomania."

The individual who could excite such lively enthusiasm was simply a bookbinder, but of such eminence in his art, as to render all his works exceedingly valuable. For taste, judicious choice of ornament, and soundness of workmanship, Payne was unrivalled in his day, and some maintain that he has never been equalled in subsequent times. But whatever lustre Roger may have diffused, it was by his handiwork alone; in person he was a filthy, ragged, ale-sodden creature, with a foolish, and even fierce indifference to the common decencies of life. His workshop was a deplorable filthy den, unapproachable by his patrons; yet, when he waited on his distinguished employers, he made no alteration in his dress. The Countess of Spencer's French maid fainted when she saw such a specimen of humanity in conversation with her mistress.

In spite of his eccentric habits, Payne might have made a fortune by his business, and ridden in a carriage, as finely decorated as the books he bound. The rock on which he split was the excessively ardent devotion which he cherished for strong ale. Ale may be said to have been meat, drink, washing, and lodging for the wretched Roger. When remonstrated with by his friends and patrons, and told that sobriety, like honesty, was the best policy, and the only road that led to health and wealth, he would reply by chanting a verse of an old song in praise of his favourite beverage, thus:

All history gathers
From ancient forefathers,
That ale's the true liquor of life;
Men lived long in health,
And preserved their wealth,
Whilst barley-broth only was rife.

Roger described his fine workmanship in a bill for binding presented to Dr. Mosely, his personal physician:

"*Harmony of the World, by Haydon: London 1642.* Bound in the very best manner; the book sewed in the very best manner with white silk, very strong, and will open easy; very neat and strong boards; fine drawing-paper inside stained to suit the colour of the book. The outsides finished in the *Rose-Crucian taste* — very correct measured work. The inside finished in the *Druid taste*, with *Acorns* and *SS*. studded with *Stars*, &c., in the most magnificent manner. So neat, strong, and elegant as this book is bound, the binding is well worth 13s., and the inlaying the frontispiece, cleaning and mending, is worth 2s. To Dr. Mosely's great goodness, I am so much indebted, that my gratitude sets the price for binding, inlaying, cleaning, and mending at only . . . £0 10 6"

(Roger Payne died peacefully drunk in 1797.)

— R. Chambers, *The Book of Days*

A binder at his ease. (The Bettmann Archive, New York.)

How many a man has dated a new era in his life from the reading of a book.
— Henry David Thoreau (1817-1862)

The First Printed Book

The first attempts at mechanical printing featured each page carved in reverse on a solid block of wood which was then pressed against the paper. But the blocks quickly broke and new letters would have to be carved and glued into position. From this state of affairs came the idea of carving each letter separately. This movable type could be easily assembled to form each page of a book and if produced in metal the letters would last for many impressions.

Several printers in Europe were working on these ideas but in 1450 Johann Gutenberg was keen enough to borrow money from Johann Faust to perfect his conception of a printing press. But when no book had appeared from Gutenberg's press five years later, Faust sued for his money and bankrupted Gutenberg. Then, with Peter Schoeffer, a type designer, Faust brought out the first printed book in Mainz, Germany, in 1456. But Johann Gutenberg had the last word in the matter. The book is known as the Gutenberg Bible.

A page from the first printed book.

The Most Expensive Book in the World

Three copies of the Gutenberg Bible changed hands in 1978. In March, the Gutenberg Museum in Mainz, Germany, paid $1,800,000 for a single copy. One month later, the West German Library in Stuttgart paid $2,000,000 for another. In June, the University of Texas bought a Gutenberg Bible for $2,400,000, the highest price ever known to have been paid for a book.

The Importance of the Printer

The printer is the friend of intelligence, of thought; he is the friend of liberty, of freedom, of law; indeed, the printer is the friend of every man who is the friend of order — the friend of every man who can read. Of all the inventions, of all the discoveries in science or art, of all the great results in the wonderful progress of mechanical energy and skill, the printer is the only product of civilization necessary to the existence of free man.

— Charles Dickens (1812–1870)

The First Book Printed in England

The introduction of printing into England is undoubtedly to be ascribed to William Caxton, a modest, worthy, and industrious man, who went to Germany entirely to learn the art; and having practised it himself at Cologne, in 1471, brought it to England two years afterwards. He was not only a printer, but an author; and the book which he translated, called the *Game and Playe of the Chesse*, and which appeared in 1474, is considered as the first production of the English press.

— William Keddie, *Anecdotes Literary and Scientific*

The First Book Printed in North America

In Cambridge, Massachusetts, Stephen Daye, a locksmith by trade, took over the printing press brought to the New World by the Reverend Jose Glover who had died. In 1640, Mr. Daye printed 1,700 copies of what is commonly known as the *Bay Psalm Book*, though its full title is *The Whole Booke of Psalms Faithfully Translated Into English Metre.*

The second part of the history of the world and the arts begins with the invention of printing.

— Johann Wolfgang Goethe (1749-1832)

The Most Valuable Book in English?

Today, the Bay Psalm Book may be the most valuable in the English language. Only eleven copies are known to exist, with nine of them defective. The last public sale of a copy took place on January 28, 1947, at the Parke-Bernet Galleries in New York when the Yale University Library paid $151,000. Collectors believe the next sale will surely realize over $1,000,000 for the small 147-page, roughly printed book.

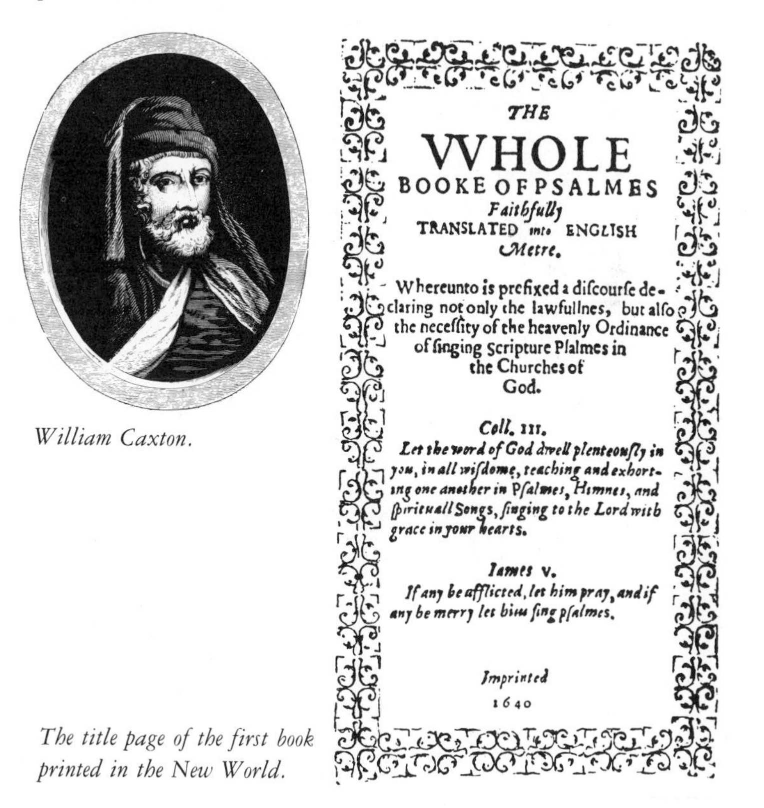

THE

VVHOLE

BOOKE OF PSALMES

Faithfully

TRANSLATED *into* ENGLISH

Metre.

Whereunto is prefixed a diſcourſe declaring not only the lawfullnes, but alſo the neceſſity of the heavenly Ordinance of ſinging Scripture Pſalmes in the Churches of God.

Coll. III.

Let the word of God dwell plenteouſly in you, in all wiſdome, teaching and exhorting one another in Pſalmes, Himnes, and ſpirituall Songs, ſinging to the Lord with grace in your hearts.

Iames V.

If any be afflicted, let him pray, and if any be merry let him ſing pſalmes.

Imprinted

1640

William Caxton.

The title page of the first book printed in the New World.

No other art is more justified than typography in looking ahead to future centuries; for the creations of typography benefit coming generations as much as present ones.
— Giambattista Bodoni, 1818

A Well-preserved Typographer

John Baskerville, a native of Worcestershire, England, having acquired considerable wealth by the varnishing business at Birmingham, devoted himself to the perfection of the art of printing, more particularly in the shape of the letters. He is said to have spent six hundred pounds before he could obtain a single letter to please himself, and many thousands before he made a profit of his pursuit, which he prosecuted so ardently that he manufactured his own printing-ink, presses, moulds for casting, and all the apparatus for printing. His typography, which bears his name, is extremely beautiful, uniting the elegance of Plantin with the clearness of the Elzevirs; in his Italic letters he stands unrivalled, such freedom and perfect symmetry being in vain to be looked for among the specimens of Aldus and Colinaeus. He was a man of eccentric tastes; he had each panel of his carriage painted with a picture of his trades. He was buried in his garden in 1775 and in 1821, his remains being accidently disturbed, the leaden coffin was opened, and the body was found in a singular state of preservation — the shroud was perfect and very white, and a branch of laurel on the breast of the corpse was, though faded, entire.

— R. Chambers, *The Book of Days*

BIRMINGHAMIAE:

Typis JOHANNIS BASKERVILLE.

MDCCLVII.

Typesetting by John Baskerville in 1757.

Ben Franklin — "The Water American."

A Detestable Custom of Printers

Early in his career (circa 1745) Ben Franklin worked in a printing house in London where:
"I drank only water, the other workmen, nearly fifty in number, were great drinkers of beer. On one occasion, I carried up and down stairs a large form of types in each hand, when others carried but one in both hands. They wondered to see that the *Water American*, as they called me, was stronger than themselves who drank *strong* beer. We had an alehouse boy, who always attended in the house to supply the workmen. My companion at the press drank every day a pint before breakfast, a pint at breakfast with his bread and cheese, a pint between breakfast and dinner, a pint at dinner, a pint in the afternoon about six o'clock, and another when he had done with his day's work. I thought it a detestable custom; but it was necessary, he supposed, to drink strong beer that he might be strong to labour. I endeavoured to convince him that the bodily strength afforded by beer could only be in proportion to the grain or flour of the barley dissolved in the water of which it was made; that there was more flour in a pennyworth of bread; and therefore, if he could eat that with a pint of water, it would give him more strength than a quart of beer. He drank on, however, and had four or five shillings to pay out of his wages every Saturday night for the vile liquor; an expense I was free from. And thus these poor devils kept themselves always under."

— Benjamin Franklin (1706–1790)

The reading of all good books is like a conversation with the finest men of past centuries.
— René Descartes (1596-1650)

"St. Jerome in his Study" by Vincenzo Catena, circa 1506. (The National Gallery, London.)

You can cover a great deal of country in books.
— Andrew Lang (1844-1912)

The First Four Centuries of Book Production

In 1822, a statistician calculated that during the four centuries since the invention of printing in 1456, the number of works printed were distributed as follows:

First century	42,000
Second century	575,000
Third century	1,225,000
Fourth century	1,839,960
Total	3,681,960

Assuming that each edition averaged 300 copies, and each three volumes, it gives a grand total of 3,313,764,000 books.

— *The Bookworm* (1890)

The Top Ten Book Producing Countries

(Showing the number of titles published)

1.	U.S.A.	84,542
2.	U.S.S.R.	84,304
3.	West Germany	44,477
4.	Japan	36,066
5.	United Kingdom	34,340
6.	France	29,371
7.	Spain	24,584
8.	India	15,802
9.	Netherlands	12,557
10.	Poland	11,418

— *UNESCO Statistical Yearbook*

World Book Production Totals

(Showing the number of titles published)

1955	*1960*	*1965*	*1970*	*1975*	*1977*
269,000	332,000	426,000	521,000	568,000	608,000

— UNESCO *Statistical Yearbook* (1978–79)

The Book Race

(Showing the number of titles published in certain subjects)

Subject	*U.S.A.*	*U.S.S.R.*
1. Generalities	1,066	1,168
2. Philosophy, Psychology	1,223	950
3. Religion, Theology	1,926	150
4. Sociology, Statistics	1,867	617
5. Political Science	2,700	6,371
6. Law, Public Administration	1,639	1,060
7. Military Art	187	1,678
8. Education, Leisure	911	2,636
9. Trade, Transport	329	349
10. Ethnography, Folklore	153	—
11. Mathematics	513	1,156
12. Natural Sciences	1,728	5,474
13. Medical Sciences	2,144	2,317
14. Engineering	1,459	8,762
15. Agriculture	475	3,187
16. Domestic Science	693	182
17. Management, Administration	848	3,438
18. Planning, Architecture	—	1,132
19. Performing Arts	666	—
20. Games, Sports	825	400
21. Linguistics, Philology	—	2,241
22. Literature	6,493	7,687
23. Geography, Travel	515	577
24. History, Biography	2,332	1,383

— *UNESCO Statistical Yearbook*

Man builds no structure which outlives a book.
— Eugene Fitch Ware (1841-1911)

The Reading Room of the British Library

The largest of the more than 400 specialized libraries in London is the Reference Library of the British Museum containing over eight million books dating from the third century B.C. to the present. Its focal point is the huge domed Reading Room opened in 1857. Books beget books and one of the most influential volumes ever, *Das Kapital*, was written in the Reading Room by Karl Marx.

The reading room of the British Library, 1857.

The Library of Congress

In 1814, the British used the original books in the library at Washington as fuel to burn the Capitol. The next year the United States Congress bought 6,500 books from Thomas Jefferson to begin a new library. Today, the Library of Congress houses more than seventy six million items requiring a staff of 5,700 under the Librarian of Congress, Daniel J. Boorstin. Approximately one-quarter of this material forms one of the world's largest book collections in 468 languages.

The interior of the Library of Congress, 1856.

"St. John the Evangelist on Patmos" by Diego Velasquez, 1618. (The National Gallery, London.)

CHAPTER TWO

The Anatomy of Books

An investigation into the creative content of books (featuring some well-known writers at work and showing some of their habits, inspiration, productivity, and techniques) by way of titles, dedications, prefaces, and indexes.

The last thing one discovers in writing a book is what to put first.
— Blaise Pascal (1623-1662)

The Difficulty of Titles

Were it inquired of an ingenious writer what page of his work had occasioned his most perplexity, he would often point to the title-page. The curiosity which we there would excite, is, however, most fastidious to gratify.

It is too often with the Title of Books, as with those painted representations exhibited by the keepers of wild beasts; where, in general, the picture itself is made more striking and inviting to the eye, than the enclosed animal is always found to be.

— Isaac Disraeli, *Curiosities of Literature*

Strange Book Titles

- A Boke of Fishing with Hooke and Line, A Boke of Engines and Traps to take Polecats, Buzzards, Rats, Mice, and all other Kinds of Vermine and Beasts whatsoever (1600)
- A Quip for an upstart Courtier; or, a quaint Dispute between Velvet Breeches and Cloth Breeches, &c. (1592)
- A Check, or Reproof of Mr. Howlet's untimely screeching in her Majesty's Ear (1581)
- Pappe with an Hatchett, alias, a Fig for my Godsonne, or, crake me this Nutt, or, a Countrie Cuff, that is, a sound Box of the Eare for the Idiot Martin, to hold his Peace: seeing the Patch will take no warning; written by one that dares call a Dog a Dog.

— from the list of books in the library of John Brand, author of *Observations of Popular Antiquities* (circa 1800)

An Odd Title Competition

The staff of the British publication *The Bookseller* held a competition for the oddest book titles to appear at the Frankfurt Book Fair in 1980.

Among the entrants were: *Entertaining with Insects: The Original Guide to Insect Cookery*; *Ex Nuns: A Study of Emergent Role Passage*; *Where Do Babies Come From and How to Keep Them There*; *How to Conduct a One Day Conference On Death Education*; *How to Pick Up Women in Discos*, and *Do It Yourself Brain Surgery and Other Home Skills*.

The runners up in the competition were: *Once Upon a Dinklesbuhl*; *Rock Stars in Their Underpants* and *Eat Your House: Art Deco Guide to Self-Sufficiency*.

The previous standard had been set by a Japanese book of 1978 entitled *Proceedings of the 2nd International Work Shop on Nude Mice*, but in 1980 the winner was from the United States:*The Joy of Chickens*.

A
QVIP FOR AN VP-
ſtart Courtier:
Or,
A quaint diſpute betvveen Veluet breeches
and Cloth-breeches.
*Wherein is plainely ſet downe the diſorders
in all Eſtates and Trades.*

LONDON
Imprinted by Iohn Wolfe, and are to bee ſold at his
ſhop at Poules chayne. 1592.

An odd title of 1592.

Book Dedications

The practice of dedicating books has now little meaning: at best it is only a tribute of respect or affection either to a private friend or a public character. In its origin it meant far more than this. When readers were few, writers trusted to the patronage of some great person, and the dedication was the means of recommending a book to his protection, or of expressing that gratitude which was a lively sense of favors to come. Antoine Furetière, the French lexicographer, said that the inventor of dedications must certainly have been a beggar; and Edward Young agrees with him:

All other trades demand, — verse-makers beg;
A dedication is a wooden leg.

That inventor's name, however, is lost in the twilight of antiquity. The old Romans — Horace, Virgil, Cicero, Lucretius — all dedicated their works to some friend or patron. He, in return, was expected to render some equivalent in coin or kind.

Traces of the old system still lingered in Laurence Stern's time (1713–68), to add point to the dedicatory jest in his "Tristram Shandy," where the accustomed page was left blank but for the inscription "To be let or sold for fifty guineas." In 1815 a Scottish author, to a book that passed through at least three editions, prefixed a dedication as grovelling and abject as the worst example in the very worst periods of authorial servility:

To the Right Honorable the Earl of Breadalbane. May it please your lordship, with overpowering sentiments of the most profound humility I prostrate myself at your noble feet, while I offer to your lordship's high consideration those very feeble attempts to describe the indescribable and ineffable beauties of your lordship's delicious estate of Edinample. With tumid emotions of heart-distending pride, and with fervescent feelings of gratitude, I beg leave to acknowledge the honor I have to serve so noble a master, and the many advantages which I, in common with your lordship's other menials, enjoy from the exuberance of your princely liberality. That your lordship may long shine with refulgent brilliancy in the exalted station to which Providence has raised you, and that your noble family, like a bright constellation, may diffuse a splendor and glory through the high sphere of their attraction, is the fervent prayer of your lordship's most humble and most devoted servant. — .

— William S. Walsh, *A Handy-Book of Literary Curiosities*

May this volume continue in motion,
And its pages each day be unfurl'd,
Till an ant has drunk up the ocean,
Or a tortoise has crawl'd round the world.

— *Book-Verse*

High-flown Dedications

"What is done by several seemingly great and wise men, who with a new-fashioned modesty employ some paltry orator or scribbling poet, whom they bribe to flatter them with some high-flown character that shall consist of mere lies and shams, and yet the persons thus extolled shall bristle up, and peacock-like bespread their plumes, while the impudent parasite magnifies the poor wretch to the skies, and proposes him as complete pattern of all virtues, from each of which he is yet as far distant as heaven itself from hell: what is all this in the mean while but the tricking up a daw in stolen feathers, a labouring to change the black-a-moor's hue, and the drawing on a pigmy's frock over the shoulders of a giant."

— Desiderius Erasmus (1466–1530), *The Praise of Folly*

The best time for planning a book is while you're doing the dishes.
— Agatha Christie (1890-1976)

A preface, being the entrance to a book, should invite by its beauty. An elegant porch announces the splendour of the interior. For my part I always gather amusement from a preface, be it awkwardly or skilfully written; for dullness, or impertinence, may raise a laugh for a page or two. A preface is frequently a superior composition to the work itself: for, long before the days of Dr. Johnson, it had been a custom for many authors to solicit for this department of their work the ornamental contribution of a man of genius. Cicero tells his friend Atticus, that he had a volume of prefaces or introductions always ready by him to be used as circumstances required.

A good preface is as essential to put the reader into good humour, as a good prologue is to a play, or a fine symphony to an opera, containing something analogous to the work itself; so that we may feel its want as a desire not elsewhere to be gratified. The Italians call the preface *La salsa del libro*, the sauce of the book, and if well seasoned it creates an appetite in the reader to devour the book itself. A preface badly composed prejudices the reader against the work. Authors are not equally fortunate in these little introductions; some can compose volumes more skilfully than prefaces, and others can finish a preface who could never be capable of finishing a book.

On a very elegant preface prefixed to an ill-written book, it was observed that they ought never to have *come together*; but a sarcastic wit remarked that he considered such *marriages* were allowable, for they were *not of kin*.

— Isaac Disraeli, *Curiosities of Literature*

A page from the Bentivoglio Hours, *circa 1500. (Victoria & Albert Museum, London.)*

On a Pen

In youth exalted high in air,
Or bathing in the waters fair,
Nature to form me took delight,
And clad my body all in white.
My person tall, and slender waist,
On either side with fringes graced;
Till me that tyrant man espied,
And dragg'd me from my mother's side;
No wonder now I look so thin;
The tyrant stript me to the skin:
My skin he flay'd, my hair he cropt:
At head and foot my body lopt:
And then, with heart more hard than stone,
He pick'd my marrow from the bone.
To vex me more, he took a freak
To slit my tongue and make me speak:
But, that which wonderful appears,
I speak to eyes, and not to ears.
He oft employs me in disguise,
And makes me tell a thousand lies:
To me he chiefly gives in trust
To please his malice or his lust.
From me no secret he can hide:
I see his vanity and pride:
And my delight is to expose
His follies to his greatest foes.

All languages I can command,
Yet not a word I understand.
Without my aid, the best divine
In learning would not know a line:
The lawyer must forget his pleading;
The scholar could not show his reading.
Nay; man my master is my slave;
I give command to kill or save.
Can grant ten thousand pounds a-year,
And make a beggar's brat a peer.
But, while I thus my life relate,
I only hasten on my fate.
My tongue is black, my mouth is furr'd,
I hardly now can force a word.
I die unpitied and forgot,
And on some dunghill left to rot.

— An enigmatic poem by Jonathan Swift and friends (Dublin, circa 1724)

The most essential gift for a good writer is a built-in shock-proof shit-detector.

— Ernest Hemingway (1899-1961)

On Ink

I am jet black, as you may see,
The son of pitch and gloomy night;
Yet all that know me will agree,
I'm dead except I live in light.

Sometimes in panegyric high,
Like lofty Pindar, I can soar,
And raise a virgin to the sky,
Or sink her to a filthy whore.

My blood this day is very sweet,
To-morrow of a bitter juice;
Like milk, 'tis cried about the street,
And so applied to different use.

Most wondrous is my magic power;
For with one color I can paint;
I'll make the devil a saint this hour,
Next make a devil of a saint.

Through distant regions I can fly,
Provide me but with paper wings;
And fairly show a reason why
There should be quarrels among kings;

And, after all, you'll think it odd,
When learned doctors will dispute,
That I should point the word of God,
And show where they can best confute.

Let lawyers bawl and strain their throats:
'Tis I that must the lands convey,
And strip their clients to their coats;
Nay, give their very souls away.

— An enigmatic poem by Jonathan Swift and friends (Dublin, circa 1724)

I love being a writer. What I can't stand is the paperwork.
— Peter De Vries

The Joy of Writing

And now the most beautiful dawn that mortal can behold, arose upon his spirit — the dawn of a new composition. For the book that a person is beginning to create or design, contains within itself half a life, and God only knows what an expanse of futurity also. Hopes of improvement — ideas which are to ensure the development and enlightenment of the human race — swarm with a joyful vitality in his brain, as he softly paces up and down in the twilight when it has become too dark to write.

— Jean Paul Francois Richter (1763–1825)

Invention depends on patience; contemplate your subject long; it will gradually unfold, till a sort of electric spark convulses for a moment the brain, and spreads down to the very heart a glow of irritation. Then come the luxuries of genius! the true hours for production and composition; hours so delightful that I have spent twelve and fourteen successively at my writing desk, and still been in a state of pleasure.

— George Louis Lederc Buffon (1707–1788)

Training to Be a Writer

Once a lady who had a son of a literary bent asked me what training I should advise if he was to become a writer; and I replied: "Give him a hundred and fifty a year for five years, and tell him to go to the devil."

— Somerset Maugham (1874–1965)

The Writing Habits of Some Authors

Goethe wrote in pencil and felt like a mother hen to his poetry.

Göethe (1749–1832)

"I was so accustomed to say over a song to myself without being able to collect it again, that I sometimes rushed to the desk, and, without taking time to adjust a sheet that was lying crosswise, wrote the poem diagonally from beginning to end, without stirring from the spot. For the same reason I preferred to use a pencil, which gives the characters more willingly; for it had sometimes happened that the scratching and spattering of the pen would wake me from my somnambulistic poetizing, distract my attention, and stifle some small product in the birth. For such poetry I had a special reverence. My relation to it was something like a hen to the chickens, which, being fully hatched, she sees chirping about her."

My purpose is to entertain myself first and other people secondly.
— John D. MacDonald

Sir Walter Scott (1771–1832)

He rose by five o'clock, lit his own fire, when the season required one, and shaved and dressed with great deliberation; for he was a very martinet as to all but the mere coxcombries of the toilet, not abhorring effeminate dandyism itself so cordially as the slightest approach to personal slovenliness, or even those "bed-gown and slipper tricks," as he called them, in which literary men are so apt to indulge. He was seated at his desk by six o'clock, all his papers arranged before him in the most accurate order, and his books of reference marshalled around him on the floor, while at least one favourite dog lay watching his eye just beyond the line of circumvallation. Thus, by the time the family assembled for breakfast, between nine and ten, he had done enough, in his own language, "to break the neck of the day's work." After breakfast a couple of hours more were given to his solitary tasks, and by noon he was, as he used to say, his "own man." Walter Scott

Voltaire (1694–1778)

His person was that of a skeleton; but this skeleton, this combination of skin and bone, had a look of more spirit and vivacity than is generally produced by flesh and blood, however blooming and youthful. The most piercing eyes ever beheld were those of Voltaire. His whole countenance was expressive of genius, observation, and extreme sensibility. An air of irony never entirely forsook his face, but was always observed lurking in his features, whether he frowned or smiled. By far the greatest part of his time was spent in his study, and whether he read himself, or listened to another, he always had a pen in his hand, to take down notes or make remarks. Composition was his principal amusement. No author who wrote for daily bread, no young poet ardent for distinction was more assiduous with his pen, or more anxious for fresh fame, than the wealthy and applauded Voltaire. Voltaire

—William Keddie, *Anecdotes Literary and Scientific*

The tools I need for my trade are paper, tobacco, food, and a little whisky.
— William Faulkner (1897-1962)

Gin, Ale, Midnight Oil, and Other Inspirations

Sir Isaac Newton and Sir William Hamilton could write as well at noonday on the crowded thoroughfare as they could at that mysterious hour betwixt night and morning when the burning of the "midnight oil" is supposed to have such a salutary effect upon the readings and writings of poets and philosophers.

Alfred de Musset wrote lyrics and *chansons* upon the corner of a table in an ale-vault, surrounded by boisterous, rollicking companions, as easily as he might have done in the privacy of his own study. But these exceptional cases do not prove the busy street and the noisy beer-salon to be the best places for the pursuit of reading or writing. The fact that Lord Byron wrote *Don Juan* on gin and water, whilst undressing, after returning from balls and suppers one winter in Venice, only proves that Lord Byron could write brilliantly at any time, even though tipsy on gin, and half dead with exhaustion.

Sir Walter Scott, in his early years of authorship, wrote at night; but later on he reversed his plan, and wrote most of his novels before breakfast in the morning. Göethe wrote *Faust* in the morning, and almost all of Longfellow's writings were the result of morning work.

Georges Sand rose at three o'clock in the afternoon; and what with botanizing, physical exercise, receiving and calling, she passed the time until twelve o'clock at night, when she entered her library, and wrote until six in the morning, at which hour she retired to rest. It is more than possible that there was a method in her alleged madness, as there was in the ridiculed habits of the French historian, Mezeray, who used to shut himself out from the sunlight, and study at noonday by the light of candles.

Jonathan Edwards thought out his best polemical works on horseback, and John Calvin wove the fabric of his celebrated theology while in bed.

— J.C. Van Dyke, *Books and How to Use Them*

A Prolific Playwright

Lope Félix de Vega Carpio, usually known as Lope de Vega, the Spanish dramatist of the sixteenth and seventeenth centuries, was probably the most prolific literary writer that ever lived. Before his death on August 26, 1653, he wrote over 1,800 plays. Most of them were three-act comedies in verse, and it was said of him that he needed only twenty four hours, when pushed, to complete one. On one occasion, at Toledo, he wrote five plays in two weeks. It has been calculated that his total production was about 21,300,000 verses.

A Voluminous Author

Dr. Cotton Mather, who died in Boston in 1728, was a man of unequalled industry, vast learning, and most disinterested benevolence. No person in America had at that time so large a library, or had read so many books, or had retained so much of what they had read. It was his custom to read fifteen chapters in the Bible every day. He wrote over his study door, in capital letters, "Be Short." In one year he kept sixty fasts and twenty vigils, and published fourteen books. His publications amounted in all to 382, some of them being of huge dimensions. His *Magnalia* was the largest; it consisted of seven folio volumes.

— William Keddie, *Anecdotes Literary and Scientific*

Begin every story in the middle. The reader doesn't care how it begins, he wants to get on with it.

— Louis L'Amour

A Creative Cobbler

Hans Sachs of Nurnberg, Germany, dabbled in authorship when not practising his trade of shoemaker. During his lifetime (1494–1578), he cobbled up fifty-three sacred and seventy-eight profane dramas, sixty-four farces, fifty-nine fables, and over six-thousand poetical pieces.

200,000,000 Books

As of early 1980, the English author Barbara Cartland, whose heroine is always a virgin, and Louis L'Amour who has written seventy-six novels about American cowboys, had each sold over one hundred million books. From 1948 to 1981 the fifteen novels of Harold Robbins have sold over 200,000,000 copies. An estimated 40,000 are sold every day.

It took me fifteen years to discover I had no talent for writing, but I couldn't give it up because by that time I was too famous.
— Robert Benchley (1889-1945)

A Grub Street Hack

Without formal petition
Thus stands my condition:
I am closely blocked up in a garret,
Where I scribble and smoke,
And sadly invoke
The powerful assistance of claret.
Four children and a wife,
'Tis hard on my life,
Beside myself and a muse,
To be all clothed and fed,
Now the times are so dead,
By my scribbling of doggerel and news.
And what shall I do,
I'm a wretch if I know,
So hard is the fate of a poet;
I must either turn rogue,
Or, what's as bad, pedagogue,
And so drudge like a thing that has no wit.
My levee's all duns,
Attended by bums,
And my landlady too she's a teaser,
At least four times a day
She warns me away,
And what can a man do to please her?
Here's the victualler and vintner,
The cook and the printer,
With their myrmidons hovering about, sir;
The tailor and draper,
With the cur that sells paper,
That, in short, I dare not stir out, sir,
But my books sure may go,
My master Ovid's did so,
And tell how doleful the case is;
If I don't move your pity,
To make short of my ditty,
'Twill serve you to wipe your arses.

— Tom Brown (1663–1704), *The Poet's Condition*

Grub Street, London, where the hacks wrote.

Hack Writers in Grub Street

In the late seventeenth and early eighteenth centuries in London, many impoverished writers cranked out pamphlets and books on an assembly line basis for the flourishing trade in trashy literature. Henry Fielding describes one such situation in the back of a bookseller's shop in Grub Street:

BOOKSELLER: Fie upon it, gentlemen! — what, not at your pens? Do you consider, Mr. Quibble, that it is above a fortnight since your *Letter from a Friend in the Country* was published? Is it not high time for an answer to come out? At this rate, before your answer is printed, your book will be forgot: I love to keep a controversy up warm. I have had authors who have writ a book in the morning, answered it in the afternoon, and compromised the matter at night.

QUIBBLE: Sir, I will be as expeditious as possible.

BOOKSELLER: Well, Mr. Dash, have you done that murder yet?

DASH: Yes, sir; the murder is done, I am only about a few moral reflections to place before it.

BOOKSELLER: Very well; then let me have a ghost finished by this day seven-night.

DASH: What sort of ghost would you have, sir? The last was a pale one.

BOOKSELLER: Then let this be a bloody one.

— Henry Fielding, *Author's Farce* (1730)

I can't understand why a person will take a year or two to write a novel when he can easily buy one for a few dollars.
— Fred Allen (1894-1956)

Advice to a Would-be Author

You ask me, friend and neighbour,
For a record of my labour —
('Tis the pen and not the sabre
Is the weapon that I wield) —
You want to get the *gist* of
The stuff my works *consist* of,
Which I'll try to give a *list* of,
From the time I took the field.

In years of youth and leisure
My ink-pot seem'd a treasure,
I knew an author's pleasure,
And experienced his pain;
When fluently he scribbles,
Or his quill in anguish nibbles,
As the stream of fancy dribbles
Slow and sluggish through his brain.

I early took to writing
About mediaeval fighting.
By paladins delighting
In the most chivalric names;
I know not of the *gain's* worth,
One tithe of what the *pain's* worth,
But I've imitated *Ains*worth
And I've copied Scott and James.

I've written of the Ocean
With a semblance of devotion,
(Though I'm sickly with the motion
If I venture on a ship) —
Of pirate fights and struggles,
And how the man who smuggles
Manoeuvres, plans, and juggles
To give his foes the slip.

Oft, as a mental tonic,
I turn to themes Byronic,
To misanthropes sardonic,
Of reserved and lofty ways;
But I've never, never written,
In the style of Bulwer Lytton,
Of morbid creatures smitten
With a metaphysic craze.

I'm very fond of timing
My Pegasus to rhyming,
For I love the tuneful chiming
Of the vowels at the close;
So wild is oft my patter
That friends, who never flatter,
Say "you're madder than a hatter
To write such rhymes as those!"

But when it gets too fearful,
To ballads bright and cheerful,
Or tender, touching, tearful,
I tune my wayward lyre;
And sing of sweet affection,
Or of mournful recollection,
Called up by the reflection
Of faces in the fire.

Ah! friend, if you're a poet,
Though your intimates may know it,
It is very hard to show it
To the public and the press,
For readers shy at verses,
And the critic only curses,
And you won't fill many purses
With the proceeds of success.

Yet, if a person chooses
To labour for the Muses,
Although the world refuses
Encouragement to give,
I'll never blame him — never,
If he's earnest in endeavour,
Though he must be very clever
If he manages to live!

The bee, in weather sunny,
Is sure of finding honey,
And the humble hare and bunny
Get subsistence from the soil;
But a writer, grave or funny,
Whatsoever work he's *done*, he
May be void of fame and money
After twenty years of toil.

Ah! neighbour, if you knew it
(I've but hastily run through it)
There's much to make us rue it
In an author's chequered lot;
But if, when you review it,
You're tempted to pursue it,
Pray do it — or eschew it,
But I think you'd better *not*!

— Walter Parke, *Patter Poems* (1885)

One writer, for instance, excels at a plan or a title-page, another works away at the body of the book, and a third has a dab at an index.
— Oliver Goldsmith (1728-1774)

The Nerves and Arteries of a Book

"I for my part venerate the inventor of Indexes; and I know not to whom to yield the preference, either to Hippocrates, who was the great anatomiser of the human body, or to that unknown labourer in literature who first laid open the nerves and arteries of a book."

— Isaac Disraeli, *Literary Miscellanies*

Arrows into the Body of the Book

"It will thus often happen that the controversialist states his case first in the title page; he then gives it at greater length in the introduction; again perhaps in a preface; a third time in an analytical form through means of a table of contents; after all this skirmishing he brings up his heavy columns in the body of the book; and if he be very skilfull he may let fly a few Parthian arrows from the index."

— J. Hill Burton, *The Book-Hunter*

Information from the Rear

"The most accomplisht way of using books at present is twofold: Either serve them as some men do Lords, learn their titles exactly, and then brag of their acquaintance. Or secondly, which indeed is the choicer, the profounder and politer method, to get a thorough insight into the Index, by which the whole book is governed and turned, like fishes by the tail. For to enter the palace of Learning at the great gate, requires an expense of time and forms; therefore men of much haste and little ceremony are content to get in by the back door. For, the Arts are all in a flying march, and therefore more easily subdued by attacking them in the rear. . . . Thus men catch Knowledge by throwing their wit on the posteriors of a book, as boys do sparrows with flinging salt upon their tails. Thus human life is best understood by the wise man's Rule of regarding the end. Thus are the Sciences found like Hercules' oxen, by tracing them backwards. Thus are old Sciences unravelled like old stockings, by beginning at the foot. Thus physicians discover the state of the whole body by consulting only what comes from behind."

— Jonathan Swift, *A Tale of a Tub*

A Comprehensive Cockatoo

(An index without cross-references, but with the same subject listed under every conceivable heading).

Absurd tale about a Cockatoo, 136.
Anecdote, absurd one, about a Cockatoo, 136.
Bathos and a Cockatoo, 136.
Cockatoo, absurd tale concerning one, 136.
Discourse held with a Cockatoo, 136.
Incredibly absurd tale of a Cockatoo, 136.
Invalid Cockatoo, absurd tale about, 136.
Mr. R—— and tale about a Cockatoo, 136.
Preposterous tale about a Cockatoo, 136.
Questions answered by a Cockatoo, 136.
R——, Mr., and tale about a Cockatoo, 136.
Rational Cockatoo, as asserted, 136.
Tale about a rational Cockatoo, as asserted, 136.
Very absurd tale about a Cockatoo, 136.
Wonderfully foolish tale about a Cockatoo, 136.

— St. George Mivart, *Origin of Human Reason*

Cross-Purpose Cross-References

(A bad index makes it seem that the author and the indexer are playing at cross-purposes).

Cards *see* Dice.
Cattle *see* Clergy.
Chastity *see* Homicide.
Cheese *see* Butter.
Coin *see* High Treason.
Convicts *see* Clergy.
Death *see* Appeal.
Election *see* Bribery.
Farthings *see* Halfpenny.
Fear *see* Robbery.
Footway *see* Nuisance.
Honour *see* Constable.
Incapacity *see* Officers.
King *see* Treason.
Knaves *see* Words.
Letters *see* Libel.
London *see* Outlawry.
Shop *see* Burglary.
Sickness *see* Bail.
Threats *see* Words.
Writing *see* Treason.

— Sarjeant William Hawkins, *Pleas of the Crown* (1716)

Dr. Samuel Johnson.

The surest way to make a monkey of a man is to quote him. That remark in itself wouldn't make any sense if quoted as it stands.

— Robert Benchley (1889-1945)

Quotations

When a thing has been said and well said, have no scruple: take it and copy it. Give references? Why should you? Either your readers know where you have taken the passage and the precaution is needless, or they do not know and you humiliate them.

—Anatole France (1844–1924)

Bibliography

"It is by means of such Works that the Student comes to know what has been written on every part of learning; that he avoids the hazards of encountering difficulties which have already been cleared; of discussing questions which have already been decided; and of digging in mines of literature which have already been exhausted."

— Dr. Samuel Johnson (1709–84)

Sources

All these things heer collected, are not mine,
But divers grapes make but one sort of wine;
So I, from many learned authors took
The various matters printed in this book.
What's not mine own by me shall not be father'd,
The most part I in fifty years have gather'd,
Some things are very good, pick out the best,
Good wits compiled them, and I wrote the rest.
If thou dost buy it, it will quit thy cost,
Read it, and all thy labour is not lost.

— John Taylor, *Miscellanies; or Fifty Years' Gatherings out of Sundry Authors, etc.* (1652)

Chronology

"Surely these are points not wholly uninteresting or uninstructive: they are historical details which many persons may rationally desire to know, and such as no man ever needs to feel himself ashamed of knowing. If I do not here give him the most full and satisfactory intelligence on each particular, let it be remembered that at least I neither cut off nor obstruct his way to more copious sources; on the contrary, I studiously direct the inquirer to further information, wheresoever the opportunity is afforded me."

— Cotton's *Typographical Gazetteer*, Oxford (1831)

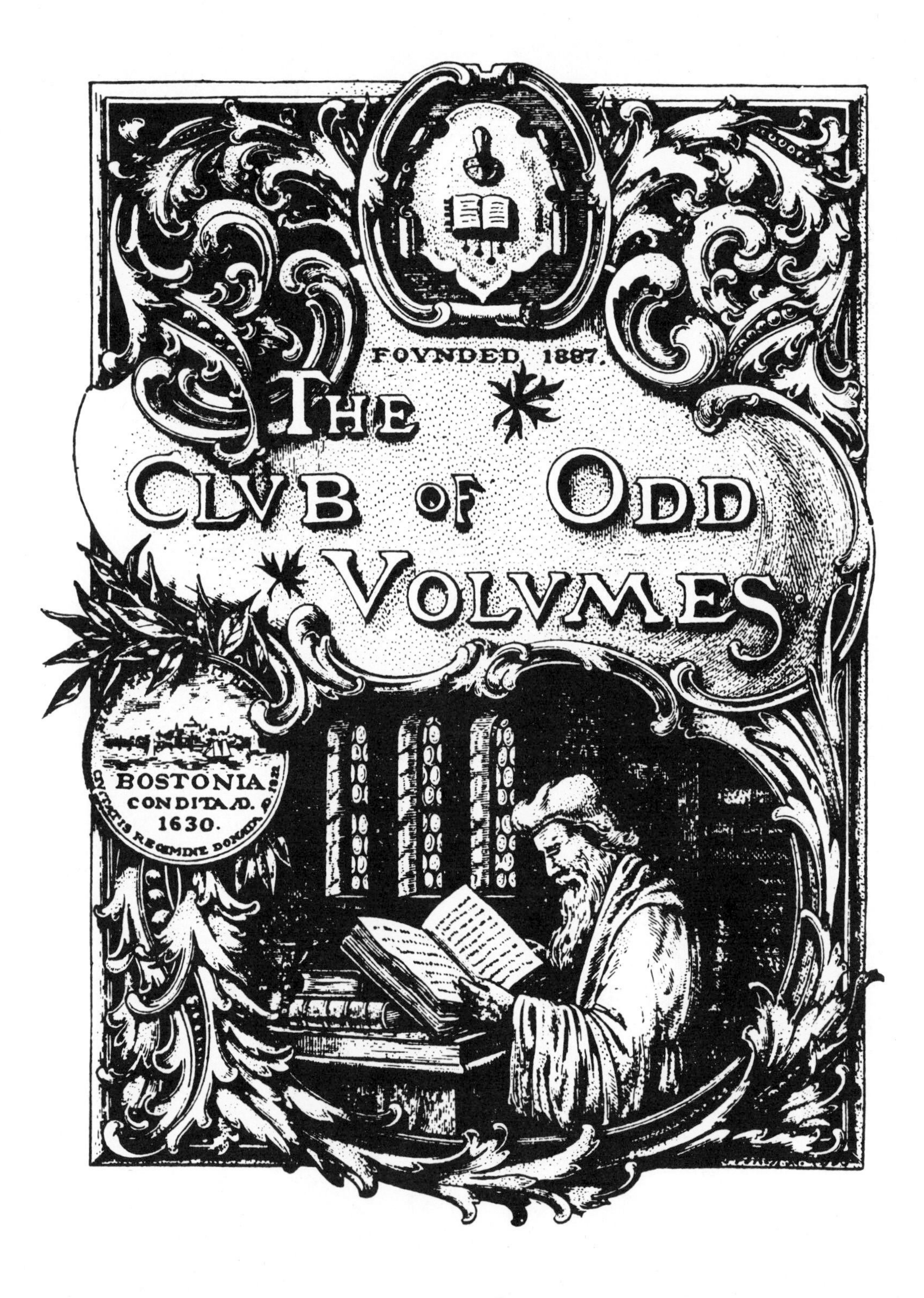
FOVNDED 1887.
THE
CLVB OF ODD
VOLVMES.
BOSTONIA
CONDITA A.D.
1630.
CIVITATIS REGIMINE DONATA

CHAPTER THREE

Book Lore

Anecdotes and curiosities concerning some famous
and infamous books, the adventures and misadventures
of certain celebrated authors with assorted literary difficulties,
earnings, epitaphs, errata, events, forgeries,
hoaxes, insights, mistakes, plagiarisms, reviews, statistics, and trivia.

Another damned, thick, square book! Always scribble, scribble, scribble! Eh! Mr. Gibbon?

— William Henry, Duke of Gloucester (1743-1805)

The Beginning and Ending of a Long Book

Edward Gibbon, author of the epic *Decline And Fall of The Roman Empire* tells how the book began and ended:

"It was at Rome, on the 15th of October 1764, as I sat musing amidst the ruins of the Capitol, while the bare-footed friars were singing vespers in the Temple of Jupiter, that the idea of writing the decline and fall of the city first started to my mind."

He began the work in 1772, and fifteen years later in Lausanne, Switzerland,

"It was on the day, or rather night, of the 27th of June 1787, between the hours of eleven and twelve, that I wrote the last lines of the last page, in a summer-house in my garden. After laying down my pen, I took several turns in a berceau, or covered walk of acacias, which commands a prospect of the country, the lake, and the mountains. The air was temperate, the sky was serene, the silver orb of the moon was reflected from the waters, and all nature was silent. I will not dissemble the first emotions of joy on recovering my freedom, and, perhaps, the establishment of my fame. But my pride was soon humbled, and a sober melancholy was spread over my mind, by the idea that I had taken an everlasting leave of an old and agreeable companion, and that whatsoever might be the future fate of my History, the life of the historian must be short and precarious."

(The historian was then fifty. He died seven years later.)

— R. Chambers, *The Book of Days*

Gibbon's house at Lausanne where the Empire fell.

Small Books

These tiny books, reproduced in their actual size, are from the lilliputian library of M. George Salomon, a nineteenth century French collector who assembled 700 volumes, none of which exceeded two inches by one and one-third inches in size. The smallest of all is the *Chemin de la Croix,* which contains 119 pages, the type in each page measuring one-half inch in height and a quarter of an inch in width.

Edward Gibbon scribbled for fifteen years on his epic book.

The Iliad in a Nutshell?

The Iliad of Homer in a nutshell, which Pliny says that Cicero once saw, it is pretended might have been a fact, however to some it may appear impossible.

One learned man trifled half an hour in demonstrating it possible. A piece of vellum, about ten inches in length and eight in width, pliant and firm, can be folded up, and enclosed in the shell of a large walnut. It can hold in its breadth one line, which can contain 30 verses, and in its length 250 lines. With a crow-quill the writing can be perfect. A page of this piece of vellum will then contain 7,500 verses, and the reverse as much; the whole 15,000 verses of the Iliad. And this he proved by using a piece of paper, and with a common pen. The thing is possible to be effected; and if on any occasion paper should be most excessively rare, it may be useful to know that a volume of matter may be contained in a single leaf.

— Isaac Disraeli, *Curiosities of Literature*

A big book is a big nuisance.
— Callimachus (circa 260 B.C.)

The Biggest Book in the World?

In 1660 the merchants of Amsterdam presented King Charles II of England with a giant atlas of the world. The book, now in the British Museum, is five feet ten inches high by three feet six inches wide, and runs on wheels when opened.

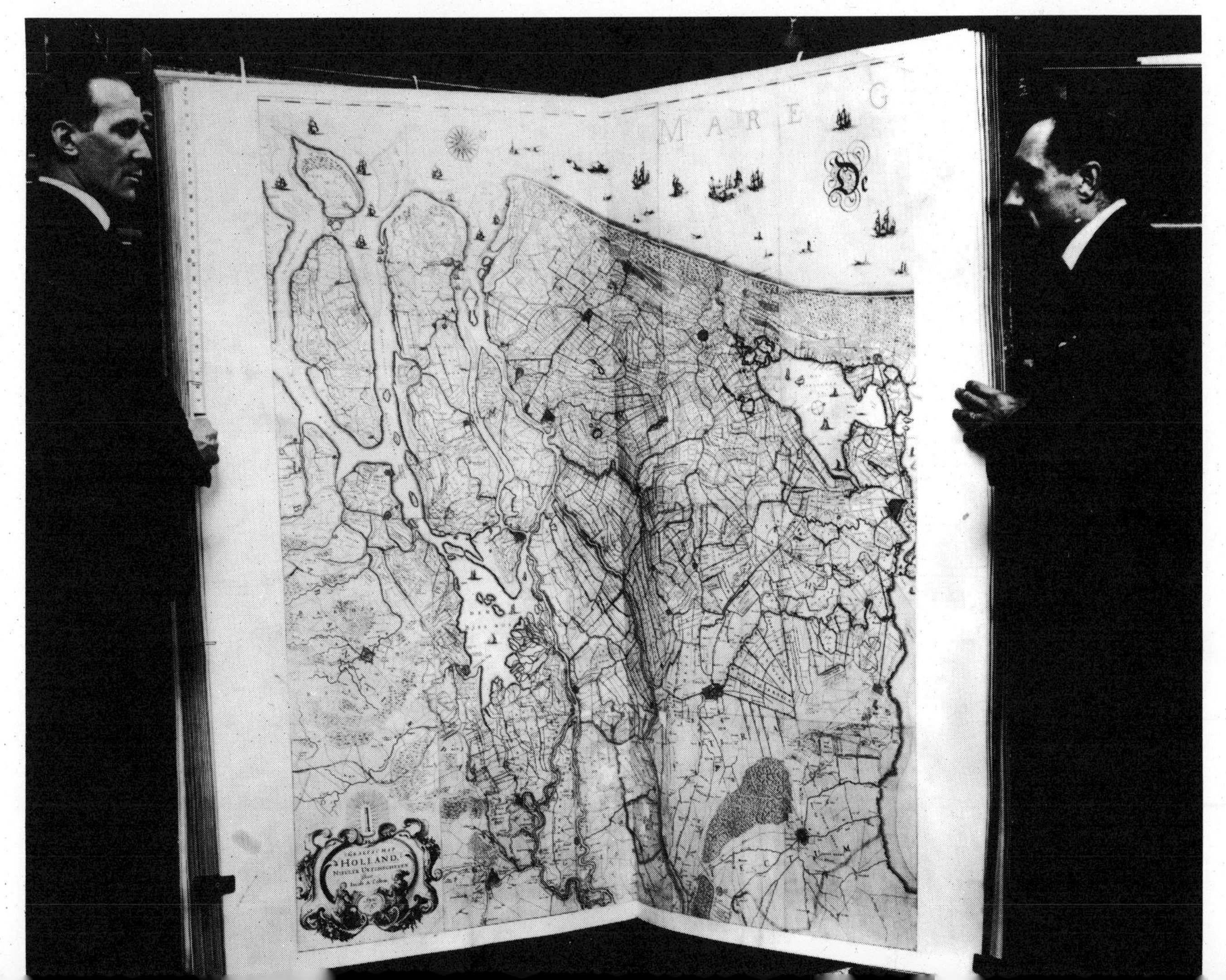

Many thanks; I shall lose no time in reading it.
— Benjamin Disraeli (1804-1881) on receiving unsolicited manuscripts.

Some Rejection Slips

In works of fiction, perhaps the most notable example of a story which was offered to publisher after publisher only to be returned to its author, Daniel Defoe, is that of *Robinson Crusoe*. It was at last "Printed for W. Taylor, at the Ship in Paternoster Row, MDCCXIX."

Jane Austen's name stands high in the annals of English literature; yet she had a struggle to get her books published. She sold her *Northanger Abbey* to a Bath bookseller for the insignificant sum of ten pounds. The manuscript remained for some time in his possession without being printed, he fearing that if published it would prove a failure.

William Makepeace Thackeray wrote his great novel *Vanity Fair*, for *Colburn's Magazine*; it was refused by the publishers, who deemed it a work without interest. He tried to place it with several of the leading London firms who all declined it. He finally published it himself in monthly parts.

The first volume of Hans Christian Andersen's *Fairy Tales* was declined by every publisher in Copenhagen. The book was brought out at the author's own cost.

Harriet Beecher Stowe's *Uncle Tom's Cabin* was written as a serial for the *National Era*, an anti-slavery journal published at Washington. It was next offered to Messrs. Jewett & Co., but their reader and critic pronounced it not a story of sufficient interest to be worth reproducing in book form. The wife of the latter strenuously insisted that it would meet with favourable reception, and advised its publication.

— William Andrews, *Literary Byways*

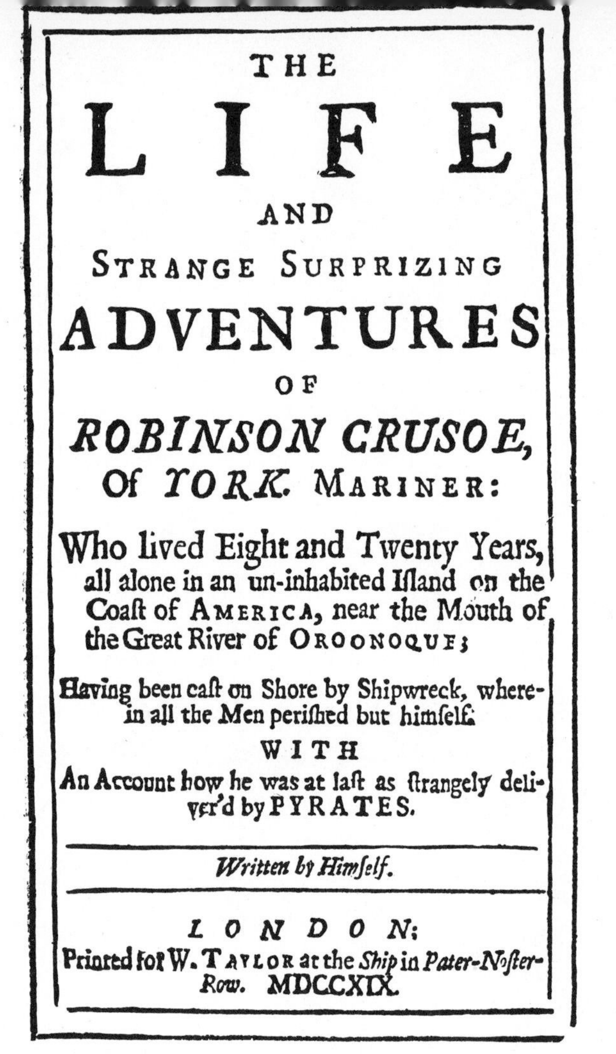
THE
LIFE
AND
STRANGE SURPRIZING
ADVENTURES
OF
ROBINSON CRUSOE,
Of *YORK*, MARINER:
Who lived Eight and Twenty Years, all alone in an un-inhabited Island on the Coast of AMERICA, near the Mouth of the Great River of OROONOQUE;
Having been cast on Shore by Shipwreck, wherein all the Men perished but himself.
WITH
An Account how he was at last as strangely deliver'd by PYRATES.

Written by Himself.

LONDON:
Printed for W. TAYLOR at the *Ship* in *Pater-Noster-Row*. MDCCXIX.

The title page of the first edition of Robinson Crusoe.

Dictionary Difficulties

Though Noah Webster (1758–1843) eventually found a publisher for his dictionary, the American lexicographer had difficulty in the beginning.

In a letter written from London in 1825, he says that he had tried for several weeks unsuccessfully to find a purchaser for his dictionary. The booksellers gave him various reasons for declining to produce his work, except one gentleman who refused to assign any reason at all. "I know not what I shall ultimately do," says the unfortunate author. "The gentlemen who have examined a portion of the manuscript think well of it, and one bookseller says explicitly the work will maintain its ground, but how to get it published I do not know."

— *The Bookworm*

Belated Bestsellers in China

In February of 1978, a queue 100 yards long formed outside a bookshop in Peking. The eager customers were lined up to purchase copies (at the equivalent of twenty cents each) of the Chinese version of Shakespeare, the first to appear in that country for twenty-three years. *Love Story* and *The Catcher in the Rye* also sold well.

Paperback Millionaires

In recent years certain books have commanded fabulous prices in bidding wars between rival publishers vying for the rights to publish them in paperback. Although the authors don't receive all of the money, the following ladies have become very wealthy from these books:
The Thorn Birds by Colleen McCullough, Avon Books (1978) — $1,900,000.
The Bleeding Heart by Marilyn French, Ballantine Books (1979) — $1,900,000.
Love Signs by Linda Goodman, Fawcett Books (1978) — $2,250,000.
Princess Daisy by Judith Krantz, Bantam Books, (1979) — $3,208,875.

A High-priced Poem

Jacopo Sannazaro, an Italian poet, died in Naples in the year 1458. Among the highest sums ever paid for poetical composition were the 6,000 golden crowns given to him by the citizens of Venice for his six eulogistical lines on their city:
Neptune saw Venus on the Adria stand
Firm as a rock, and all the sea command,
"Think'st thou, O Jove!" said he, "Rome's walls excel?
Or that proud cliffe, whence false Tarpei fell?
Grant Tiber best, view both; and you will say,
That men did those, god these foundations lay."

The Top Twenty Authors in the World (1974)

(Based on those most frequently translated and showing the author, home country and number of translations).

1.	V.I. Lenin	U.S.S.R.	401
2.	Karl Marx	Germany	196
3.	Jules Verne	France	164
4.	E. Blyton	U.K.	149
5.	L.I. Brezhnev	U.S.S.R.	149
6.	A. Christie	U.K.	136
7.	J. London	U.S.A.	130
8.	W. Disney	U.S.A.	110
9.	W. Shakespeare	U.K.	97
10.	M. Gorky	U.S.S.R.	92
11.	P.S. Buck	U.S.A.	90
12.	G. Simenon	Belgium	88
13.	A. Solzhenitsyn	U.S.S.R.	88
14.	F.M. Dostoevsky	U.S.S.R.	86
15.	J.W. Grimm	Germany	85
16.	A. Maclean	U.K.	85
17.	F.W. Dixon	U.S.A.	83
18.	L.N. Tolstoy	U.S.S.R.	74
19.	E. Hemingway	U.S.A.	73
20.	M. Twain	U.S.A.	69

(There were 286 translations of the Bible in 1974.)

— *UNESCO Statistical Yearbook (1978–9)*

No man but a blockhead ever wrote, except for money.
— Samuel Johnson (1709-1784)

Some Authors' Earnings

(in the currency of their time)
Hamlet, William Shakespeare — £5
Paradise Lost, John Milton — £5
Northanger Abbey, Jane Austen — £10
The Vicar of Wakefield, Oliver Goldsmith — £60
The Beggar's Opera, John Gay — £400
Tom Jones, Henry Fielding — £700
English Dictionary, Dr. Samuel Johnson — £1575
The Lady of the Lake, Walter Scott — £2100
Lala Rookh, Thomas Moore — £3000
Phineas Finn, Anthony Trollope — £3200
Decline And Fall of the Roman Empire, Edward Gibbon — $10,000
Adam Bede, George Eliot — £40,000
The Village Blacksmith, Henry Wadsworth Longfellow — $15

— William Andrews, *Literary Byways*

Even the best writers talk too much.
— Marquis De Vauvenargues (1715-1747)

A Wordy Author

(Charles Lamb, 1775–1834, speaking of Samuel Taylor Coleridge, 1772–1834)

"I was going from my house at Enfield to the India House one morning, and was hurrying, for I was rather late, when I met Coleridge, on his way to pay me a visit. He was brimful of some new idea, and in spite of my assuring him that time was precious, he drew me within the door of an unoccupied garden by the roadside, and there, sheltered from observation by a hedge of evergreens, he took me by the button of my coat and closing his eyes, commenced an eloquent discourse, waving his right hand gently, as the musical words flowed in an unbroken stream from his lips. I listened entranced; but the striking of a church clock recalled me to a sense of duty. I saw it was of no use to attempt to break away, so taking advantage of his absorption in his subject, I, with my penknife, quietly severed the button from my coat and decamped. Five hours afterwards, in passing the same garden, on my way home, I heard Coleridge's voice, and on looking in, there he was, with closed eyes — the button in his fingers — and his right hand gracefully waving, just as when I left him. He had never missed me!"

— J.R. Rees, *The Diversions of A Book-Worm*

Charles Lamb used a knife to escape from Coleridge.

Shelley's Strange Amusement

Percy Bysshe Shelley who, ironically, died by drowning in 1822, had a pleasure in making paper boats, and floating them on the water. So long as his paper lasted, he remained rivetted to the spot, fascinated by this peculiar amusement; all waste-paper was rapidly consumed, then the covers of letters, next letters of little value; the most precious contributions of the most esteemed correspondents, although eyed wistfully many times, and often returned to the pocket, were sure to be sent at last in pursuit of the former squadrons. Of the portable volumes which were the companions of his rambles, and he seldom went out without a book, the fly-leaves were commonly wanting — he had applied them as our ancestor Noah applied gopher-wood; but learning was so sacred in his eyes, that he never trespassed further upon the integrity of the copy; the work itself was always respected. He once found himself on the north bank of the Serpentine (where his wife drowned in 1816) without the materials for indulging those inclinations which the sight of water invariably inspired, for he had exhausted his supplies on the round pond in Kensington Gardens. Not a single scrap of paper could be found, save only a bank post bill for fifty pounds; he hesitated long, but yielded at last; he twisted it into a boat with the extreme refinement of his skill, and committed it with the utmost dexterity to fortune — watching its progress, if possible, with a still more intense anxiety than usual. Fortune often favours those who frankly and fully trust her; the north-east wind gently wafted the costly skiff to the south bank, where during the latter part of the voyage the venturous owner had waited its arrival with patient solicitude.

— William Keddie, *Anecdotes Literary and Scientific*

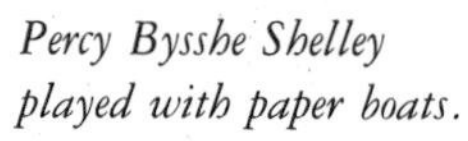

Percy Bysshe Shelley played with paper boats.

An Author and a Princess

When Honoré de Balzac (1799–1850) was at the zenith of his fame, he was travelling in Switzerland, and had arrived at an inn just at the very moment the Prince and Princess Hanski were leaving it. Balzac was ushered into the room they had just vacated, and was leaning from the window to observe their departure, when his attention was arrested by a soft voice at his elbow, asking for a book which had been left behind upon the window-seat. The lady was certainly fair, but appeared doubly so in the eyes of the poor author, when she intimated that the book she was in quest of was the pocket edition of his own works, adding that she never travelled without it, and that without it she could not exist! She drew the volume from beneath his elbow, and flew down stairs, obedient to the screaming summons of her husband — a pursy old gentleman, who was already seated in the carriage, railing in a loud voice against dilatory habits of women in general and his own spouse in particular.

For fifteen years a literary correspondence was steadily kept up between the novelist and the Princess, till at length instead of a letter containing literary strictures upon his writings, she sent an announcement of the demise of her husband the Prince — that he had bequeathed to her his domains, and his great wealth — and consequently, that she felt bound to requite him in some measure for his liberality, and had determined upon giving him a successor — in the person of de Balzac. It is needless to state that the delighted author waited not a second summons; they were forthwith united in wedlock, at her château on the Rhine, and a succession of splendid fêtes celebrated the auspicious event.

— William Keddie, *Anecdotes Literary and Scientific*

Authors in general are not good listeners.
— William Hazlitt (1778-1830)

Mark Twain's Autograph

(Twain sent a printed copy of this to anyone asking for his autograph.)

"I hope I shall not offend you; I shall certainly say nothing with the intention to offend you. I must explain myself, however, and I will do it as kindly as I can. What you ask me to do I am asked to do as often as one-half dozen times a week. Three hundred letters a year! One's impulse is to freely consent, but one's time and necessary occupations will not permit it. There is no way but to decline in all cases, making no exceptions; and I wish to call your attention to a thing which has probably not occurred to you, and that is this: that no man takes pleasure in exercising his trade as a pastime. Writing is my trade, and I exercise it only when I am obliged to. You might make your request of a doctor, or a builder, or a sculptor, and there would be no impropriety in it, but if you asked either for a specimen of his trade, his handiwork, he would be justified in rising to a point of order. It would never be fair to ask a doctor for one of his corpses to remember him by."

Pen Names

At various times during his career, Benjamin Franklin wrote under the names of Anthony Affluent, Father Abraham, Richard Saunders, Echo Proteus, Esq., The Busybody, Mrs. Silence Dogood, Philomath, and A Good Conscience.

Michael Angelo Titmarsh, Charles Yellowplush, Lancelot Wagstaff, Arthur Pendennis, George Fitz-Boodle, Peter Perseus, Jeames de la Pluche, Ikey Solomons, Jr., and Dorothea Julia Ramsbottom were in reality William Makepeace Thackeray.

Honoré de Balzac as portrayed by Gustave Doré (1833-1883), a renowned book illustrator.

Another book was opened, which is the book of life.
— Revelation, The Bible

Bible Statistics

The following facts in regard to the Authorized Version of the Bible are given by the indefatigable Dr. Horne in his "Introduction to the Study of the Scriptures." Their compilation is said to have occupied more than three years of the doctor's life:

	Old Testament	*New Testament*	*Total*
Books	39	27	66
Chapters	929	260	1,189
Verses	33,214	7,959	31,173
Words	593,493	181,253	773,746
Letters	2,728,100	838,380	3,566,480

Apocrypha

Books, 14; chapters, 183; verses, 6031; words, 125,185; letters, 1,063,876

But the good doctor's work is entirely cast into the shade by the statistical exploit of some religious enthusiast (possibly a myth), who, as a result of several years' incarceration for conscience' sake, produced this astonishing monument of misapplied industry:

The Bible contains 66 books, 1189 chapters, 33,173 verses, 773,692 words, and 3,586,489 letters. The word "and" occurs 46,227 times, the word "Lord" 1855 times, "reverend" but once, "girl" but once, in third chapter and third verse of Joel; the words "everlasting fire" but twice, and "everlasting punishment" but once. The middle line is Second Chronicles iv. 16. The middle chapter and the shortest is Psalm cxvii. The middle verse is the eighth verse of Psalm cxviii. The twenty-first verse of the seventh chapter of Ezra contains all the letters in the alphabet, except the letter "J". The finest chapter to read is the twenty-sixth chapter of the Acts of the Apostles. The nineteenth chapter of Second Kings and the thirty-seventh chapter of Isaiah are alike. The longest verse is the ninth verse of the eighth chapter of Esther. The shortest is the thirty-fifth verse of the eleventh chapter of St. John, vis: "Jesus wept." The eighth, fifteenth, twenty-first, and thirty-first verses of the 107th Psalm are alike. Each verse of the 136th Psalm ends alike. There are no words of more than six syllables.

It is evident enough that each of these tables is the result of independent labor, as they do not agree with each other as to the number of words and letters in the Bible. Probably we shall have to wait until another enthusiast is jugged before the figures are verified.

— William S. Walsh, *A Handy Book of Literary Curiosities*

Early Errata — The Devil Did It

It is said that the first book with a printed errata is the edition of *Juvenal*, with notes of Merula, printed by Gabriel Pierre, at Venice, in 1478; previously the mistakes had been corrected by the pen. One of the longest lists of errata on record, which occupies fifteen folio pages, is in the edition of the works of Picus of Mirandula, printed by Knoblauch, at Strasburg, in 1507. A worse case of blundering will be found in a little book of only one hundred and seventy-two pages, entitled *Missae ac Missalis Anatomia*, 1561, which contains fifteen pages of errata. The author, feeling that such a gross case of blundering required some excuse or explanation, accounted for the misprints by asserting that the devil drenched the manuscript in the kennel, making it almost illegible, and then obliged the printer to misread it. We may be allowed to believe that the fiend who did all the mischief was the printer's "devil."

— H.B. Wheatley, *Literary Blunders*

An Almost Perfect Book

The Foulis' editions of classical works were much prized by scholars and collectors in the nineteenth century. The celebrated Glasgow publishers once attempted to issue a book which should be a perfect specimen of typographical accuracy. Every precaution was taken to secure the desired result. Six experienced proof-readers were employed, who devoted hours to the reading of each page; and after it was thought to be perfect, it was posted up in the hall of the university, with a notification that a reward of fifty pounds would be paid to any person who could discover an error. Each page was suffered to remain two weeks in the place where it had been posted, before the work was printed, and the printers thought that they had attained the object for which they had been striving. When the work was issued, it was discovered that several errors had been committed, one of which was in the first line of the first page.

— William Keddie, *Anecdotes Literary and Scientific*

A book may be amusing with numerous errors, or it may be very dull without a single absurdity.
— Oliver Goldsmith (1728-1774)

Better Luck Next Time

"The Printer to the reader:
For errors past or faults that scaped be,
Let this collection give content to thee:
A worke of art, the grounds to us unknowne,
May cause us erre, thoughe all our skill be showne.
When points and letters, doe containe the sence,
The wise may halt, yet doe no great offence.
Then pardon here, such faults that do befall,
The next edition makes amends for all."

— A printer's note found in *The Goedeticall Staffe* by Arthur Hopton (1610)

Now wits gain praise by copying other wits
As one Hog lives on what another shits.
— Alexander Pope (1688-1744)

John Bunyan's Wit

John Bunyan (1628–1688), the Baptist preacher and author, was imprisoned in Bedford prison in the Restoration of 1660. He remained there, on and off, for twelve years. One day a Quaker called on Bunyan in jail with what he professed was a message from the Lord. "After searching for thee in half the jails of England, I am glad to have found thee at last," the man said.

"If the Lord sent thee," Bunyan replied, "you would not have needed to take so much trouble to find me out, for He knows that I have been in Bedford jail for these past seven years."

He was accused by detractors of not having written *The Pilgrim's Progress* (1678) to which he replied in verse:

It came from mine own heart, so to my head,
And thence into my fingers trickled;
Then to my pen, from whence immediately
On paper I did dribble it daintily.
Manner and matter too was all mine own,
Nor was it unto any mortal known,
Till I had done it. Nor did any then
By books, by wits, by tongues, or hand, or pen,
Add five words to it, or write half a line
Thereof: the whole and every whit is mine.

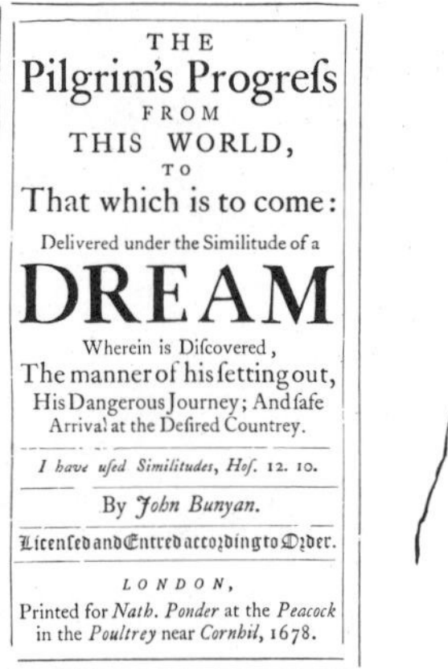

THE
Pilgrim's Progreſs
FROM
THIS WORLD,
TO
That which is to come:
Delivered under the Similitude of a
DREAM
Wherein is Diſcovered,
The manner of his ſetting out,
His Dangerous Journey; And ſafe
Arrival at the Deſired Countrey.

I have uſed Similitudes, Hoſ. 12. 10.

By *John Bunyan.*

Licenſed and Entred according to Order.

LONDON,
Printed for *Nath. Ponder* at the *Peacock* in the *Poultrey* near *Cornhil*, 1678.

JOHN • BUNYAN

Thoughts on Plagiarism

"Of all forms of theft," says Voltaire, "plagiarism is the least dangerous to society." Not only that, it is often beneficial. In mechanics all inventions are plagiarisms. If inventors had not borrowed ideas from their predecessors, progress would come to a standstill. Shall I refuse to own a timepiece because my watchmaker is not original? Shall I eschew the benefits of the modern railroad because I find the germ of the idea in the steam engine of the pre-Christian Hero? "A ship," says Emerson, "is a quotation from a forest." But inasmuch as it is not enclosed in quotation marks a ship is rank plagiarism. Shakespeare stole plots, incidents, and ideas from his forerunners. Molière derived not only his plots, but the dialogues of whole scenes, from Italian comedies. Thank God that these great men had no literary conscience! Molière openly acknowledged he had none. "I conquer my own wherever I find it," he says, with magnificent candor. And we get a new regard for Pope when we find him openly acknowledging, "I freely confess that I have served myself all I could by reading."

Mr. Cordy Jeaffreson has laid down the maxim that originality can be expected from nobody save a lunatic, a hermit, or a sensational novelist. But Andrew Lang calls this a hasty generalization. "People," he says, "will inevitably turn to these members of society (if we can speak thus of hermits and lunatics), and ask them for originality, and fail to get it, and express disappointment. For all lunatics are like other lunatics, and no more than sane men can they do anything original. As for hermits, one hermit is the very image of his brothers solitary. There remain sensational novelists to bear the brunt of the world's demand for the absolutely unheard-of, and, naturally, they cannot supply the article. So mankind falls on them, and calls them plagiarists. It is enough to make some novelists turn lunatics and others hermits."

— William S. Walsh, *A Handy-Book of Literary Curiosities*

Your comedy I've read, my friend,
And like the half you pilfered best;
Be sure the piece you yet may mend —
Take courage, man, and steal the rest.
— Anonymous

A Bogus Shakespeare

William Henry Ireland was born in London about 1776. His father, Samuel Ireland, engraved in aquatint, and published illustrated travels. This father was at the same time an amateur of old books and prints, a species of antiquary, interested particularly in whatever concerned Shakespeare, on the watch for documents and autographs.

One day in 1795 it was reported that Samuel Ireland, the engraver of Norfolk Street, was displaying manuscripts some of which were by Shakespeare's own hand, while others concerned his life and his person. He got them from his son, who, he said, had found them among some old papers in the country-seat of a neighboring gentleman. As for the name of this gentleman, the Irelands were not at liberty to make it known.

The learned world was thrown into ecstasies, men of letters, antiquaries, and curiosity-seekers flocked to Mr. Ireland's house to test the genuineness of the relics. After carefully collating the principal manuscripts with the poet's undoubted autographs, these critics expressed a firm conviction of their authenticity, and a certificate to that effect was numerously signed. A collection of rarer literary and biographic value was certainly never offered to the world. It comprised the entire manuscript of *Lear*, varying in some important respects from the printed copies; a fragment of *Hamlet*; two unpublished plays, entitled *Vortigern* and *Henry the Second*; a number of books from the poet's library, enriched with copious marginal notes; besides letters to Anne Hathaway, and others, a "Profession of Faith", legal contracts, deeds of gifts, and autograph receipts. The external evidence for the authenticity of these precious remains was pronounced by the attesting critics to be strikingly confirmed by their internal evidence. The inimitable style of the master was to be clearly discerned in the unpublished writings.

One of the learned endorsers was James Boswell, the poet-laureate who before signing the certificate of authenticity, fell upon his knees to kiss "the invaluable relics of our bard," and, "in a tone of enthusiasm and exultation, thanked God that he had lived to witness the discovery and . . . could now die in peace." And then being thirsty, he went out and drank hot brandy and water.

On the other hand, R.B. Sheridan, another man of letters, blurted forth, with an oath, "Well, Shakespeare's they may be; but if so, he was drunk when he wrote them!" But the publication of the manuscripts by subscription was soon announced. The first volume was issued in 1796, at the price of four guineas, under the editorship of Mr. Ireland.

After this publication appeared and the play *Vortigern* had a short run, the literati discovered their mistake and public ridicule forced William Ireland to make a full confession of his fraud and how he accomplished it. He procured paper by tearing out the blank leaves of old books. He was careful to soil them afterward, particularly on the edges, in order to give them an ancient air. The ink that he used was a composition which turned brown when exposed to the fire. The strings that tied his manuscripts were drawn from old tapestries. He had altered an ancient engraving, bought by chance, into a pretended portrait of Shakespeare in the character of Shylock. Unhappily for him he had but a very imperfect acquaintance with the handwriting of the poet.

— W. S. Walsh, *A Handy-Book of Literary Curiosities*

Sir, he hath never fed of the dainties that are bred in a book.
— William Shakespeare (1564-1616)

Mixed Reviews for Shakespeare

❦ The man whom nature self had made
To mock herself and Truth to imitate.

Edmund Spenser

❦ An upstart crow beautified with our feathers.

Maurice Greene

❦ I have heard that Mr. Shakespeare was a natural wit, without any art at all.

Rev. J. Ward, 1648

❦ He was honest and of an open and free nature.

Ben Jonson

❦ The merit of Shakespeare is such as the ignorant can take in and the learned add nothing to.

Dr. Samuel Johnson

❦ To him the mighty mother did unveil her awful face.

Thomas Gray

❦ But Shakespeare's magic could not copy'd be,
Within that circle none durst walk but he.

John Dryden

❦ Thou, in our wonder and astonishment,
Hath built thyself a livelong monument.

John Milton

❦ Shakespeare and Milton have had their rise, and they will have their decline.

Byron

To the Reader.

This *Figure* that thou here ſeeſt put,
It was for gentle *Shakeſpear* cut;
Wherein the *Graver* had a ſtrife
With Nature to outdo the Life.
O, could he but have drawn his Wit
As well in Braſs, as he has hit
His Face; the Print would then ſurpaſs
All that was ever writ in *Braſs*.
But ſince he cannot, Reader, look
Not on his Picture, but his *Book*.

The frontispiece of the first folio edition of Shakespeare, with an engraving by Martin Droeshout and a poem by Ben Jonson, 1623.

❦ His imperial muse tosses the creation like a bauble from hand to hand to embody any capricious thought that is uppermost in his mind.

R.W. Emerson

❦ I think most readers of Shakespeare sometimes find themselves thrown into exalted mental conditions like those produced by music. Then they may drop the book to pass at once into the region of thoughts without words.

O.W. Holmes

❦ He was master of two books unknown to many profound readers, though books which the last conflagration can alone destroy, I mean the Book of Nature and that of Man.

Edward Young

❦ His rude unpolished style and antiquated phrase and wit.

Lord Shaftesbury

❦ Was there ever such stuff as the great part of Shakespeare? Only one must not say so. But what think you? What? Is there not sad stuff? What? What?

George III

❦ You see many scenes and parts of scenes which are simply Shakespeare's disporting himself in joyous triumph and vigorous fun, after a great achievement of his highest genius.

S.T. Coleridge

❦ Shakespeare (whom you and every playhouse bill
Style the divine, the matchless, what you will),
For gain, not glory, wing'd his roving flight,
And grew immortal in his own despite.

Alexander Pope

❦ The genius of Shakespeare was an innate universality — wherefore he laid the achievement of human intellect prostrate beneath his indolent and kingly gaze.

John Keats

❦ A disproportioned and misshapen giant.

David Hume

I never read a book before reviewing it, it prejudices a man so.
— Sydney Smith (1771-1845)

Self-Criticism

How pleasant to know Mr. Lear!
Who has written such volumes of Stuff!
Some think him ill-tempered and queer,
But a few think him pleasant enough!

— Edward Lear, (1812–1888) *Nonsense Songs*

Indifferent, but Great

The four greatest novelists the world has ever known, Balzac, Dickens, Tolstoy and Dostoyevsky, wrote their respective languages very indifferently. It proves that if you can tell stories, create character, devise incidents, and if you have sincerity and passion, it doesn't matter a damn how you write.

— Somerset Maugham (1874–1965)

The Source of American Literature

All modern American literature comes from one book by Mark Twain called *Huckleberry Finn*. If you read it you must stop where the Nigger Jim is stolen from the boys. That is the real end. The rest is just cheating. But it's the best book we've had. All American writing comes from that. There was nothing before. There has been nothing as good since.

— Ernest Hemingway, *The Green Hills of Africa* (1935)

Howard Nolan, 20, an undergraduate at Brasenose College, Oxford, yesterday finished eating the 566 pages of a copy of the University Examination Statutes, which he began six days earlier.

— *London Daily Telegraph*, June 8, 1966

The Compleat Angler or the Contemplative Man's Recreation.

Being a Diſcourſe of
FISH and FISHING,
Not unworthy the peruſal of moſt *Anglers*.

Simon Peter *ſaid, I go a fiſhing: and they ſaid,* We *alſo wil go with thee. John* 21. 3.

London, Printed by *T. Maxey for Rich.* MARRIOT, *in S. Dunſtans* Church-yard, Fleet ſtreet, 1653.

The title page of the first edition of The Compleat Angler, *1653.*

A Booke Review

There is published a Booke of Eighteen-pence price, called *The Compleat Angler*, or, *The Contemplative Man's Recreation*: being a Discourse of Fish and Fishing by one Isaak Walton. Not unworthy the perusall.

— In a London newspaper, October 10, 1653

The Book-Fish

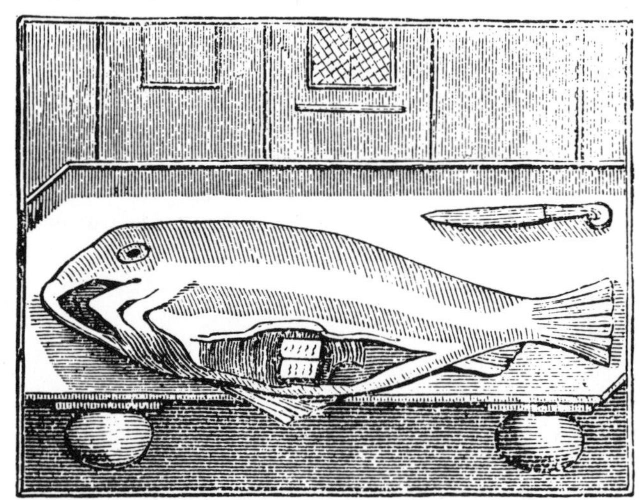

Vox Piscis *(the Book-Fish).*

On the 23rd of June 1626, a cod-fish was brought to Cambridge market, which, upon being opened, was found to contain a book in its maw or stomach. The book was much soiled, and covered with slime, though it had been wrapped in a piece of sail-cloth. It was a duodecimo work written by one John Frith, comprising several treatises on religious subjects.

The treatises contained in this book were written by Frith when in prison. Strange to say, he had been long confined in a fish cellar at Oxford, where many of his fellow-prisoners died from the impure exhalations of unsound salt fish. He was removed from thence to the Tower, and in 1533 was burned at the stake for his adherence to the reformed religion. The authorities at Cambridge reprinted the work, which had been completely forgotten, till it turned up in this strange manner. The reprint is entitled *Vox Piscis*, or the Book-Fish, and is adorned with a woodcut representing the stall in Cambridge market, with the fish, book, and knife.

— R. Chambers, *The Book of Days*

Bookish Epitaphs

Benjamin Franklin is buried beside his wife in Philadelphia, with nothing to mark the graves save this inscription on a plain slab:

Benjamin
and Franklin.
Deborah
1790.

Far more famous is the epigram which he composed upon himself, at the age of twenty-three, when a journeyman printer:

The Body
of
BENJAMIN FRANKLIN, Printer,
(Like the cover of an old book,
Its contents torn out,
And stript of its lettering and gilding,)
Lies food for worms:
Yet the work itself shall not be lost,
For it will (as he believed) appear once more,
In a new
And more beautiful edition,
Corrected and amended
by
The Author.

But this epitaph is not original. It is plagiarized from one Benjamin Woodbridge, and Woodbridge was only one in a long line of successive imitators. This gentleman was a member of the first graduating class of Harvard University, 1642. The epitaph he made upon himself is thus quoted in Cotton Mather's "Magnalia Christi Americana," a book with which Franklin was admittedly familiar:

A living, breathing Bible; tables where
Both Covenants at large engraven were.
Gospel and law, in 's heart, had each its column;
His head an index to the sacred volume;
His very name a title-page; and, next,
His life a commentary on the text.
O what a monument of glorious worth,
When, in a new edition, he comes forth!
Without errata may we think he'll be,
In leaves and covers of eternity!

— William S. Walsh, *A Handy-Book of Literary Curiosities*

When I am dead, I hope it may be said:
"His sins were scarlet, but his books were read."
— Hilaire Belloc (1870-1953)

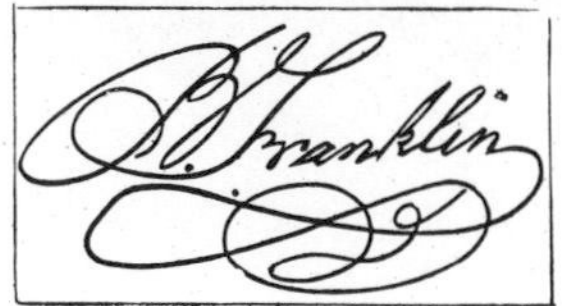

Benjamin Franklin wrote his own epitaph.

A Prolific Author's Epitaph

(Andrew Toraqueau, a teetotaler, is said to have produced a book and a child each year for twenty years.)

Here lies a man, who, drinking only water,
Wrote twenty books, with each had a son or daughter.
Had he but used the juice of generous vats,
The world would scarce have held his books and brats.

— *Book-Verse* (1896)

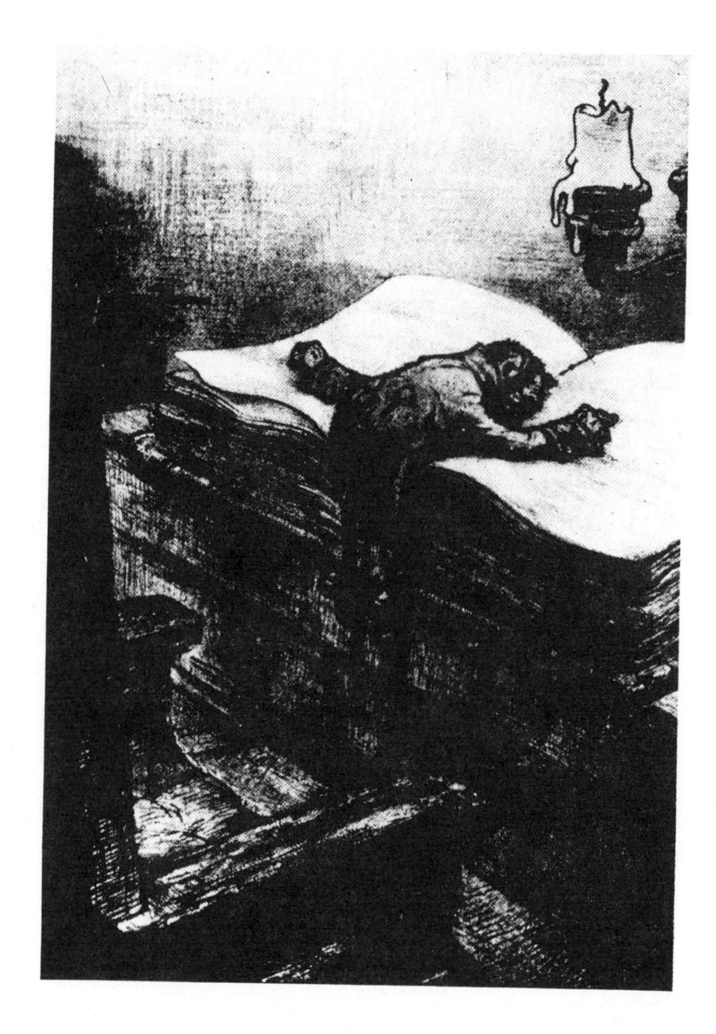

CHAPTER FOUR

Disastrous Books

The maladies, misfortunes, and sorry plights of early authors, their terrible sufferings from vicious criticisms, heartless rejections, and tragic accidents, and the appalling punishments of some literary martyrs who died for their books.

Writing a book is a horrible, exhausting struggle, like a long bout of some painful illness.
— George Orwell (1903-1950)

The Maladies of Authors

The practice of every art subjects the artist to some particular inconvenience, usually inflicting some malady on that number which has been over-wrought by excess: nature abused, pursues man into his most secret corners, and avenges herself. In the athletic exercises of the ancient Gymnasium, the pugilists were observed to become lean from their hips downwards, while the superior parts of their bodies, which they over-exercised, were prodigiously swollen; on the contrary, the racers were meagre upwards, while their feet acquired an unnatural dimension. The secret source of life seems to be carried forwards to those parts which are making the most continued efforts.

In all sedentary labours, some particular malady is contracted by every worker, derived from particular postures of the body and peculiar habits. Thus the weaver, the tailor, the painter, and the glass-blower, have all their respective maladies. The diamond-cutter, with a furnace before him, may be said almost to live in one; the slightest air must be shut out of the apartment, lest it scatter away the precious dust — a breath would ruin him!

The analogy is obvious; and the author must participate in the common fate of all sedentary occupations. But his maladies, from the very nature of the delicate organ of thinking, intensely exercised, are more terrible than those of any other profession; they are more complicated, more hidden in their causes, and the mysterious union and secret influence of the faculties of the soul over those of the body, are visible, yet still incomprehensible; they frequently produce a perturbation in the faculties, a state of acute irritability, and many sorrows and infirmities, which are not likely to create much sympathy from those around the author, who, at a glance, could have discovered where the pugilist or the racer became meagre or monstrous: the intellectual malady eludes even the tenderness of friendship.

The unnatural fixed postures, the perpetual activity of the mind, and the inaction of the body; the brain exhausted with assiduous toil deranging the nerves, vitiating the digestive powers, disordering its own machinery, and breaking the calm of sleep by that previous state of excitement which study throws us into, are some of the calamities of a studious life: for like the ocean when its swell is subsiding, the waves of the mind too still heave and beat; hence all the small feverish symptoms, and the whole train of hypochondriac affections, as well as some acute ones.

— Isaac Disraeli, *The Calamities and Quarrels of Authors*

The Plight of Authors

Authors are beings only half of earth
They own a world apart from other men:
A glorious realm, given by their fancy birth,
Subjects, a sceptre, and a diadem:
A fairy land of thought in which sweet bliss
Would run to ecstasy in wild delight —
But that stern Nature drags them back to this
With call imperious, which they may not slight:
And then they traffic with their thoughts, to live,
And coin their labouring brains for daily bread:
Getting scant dross, for the rich ore they give,
While often with the gift their life is shed!
And thus they die, leaving behind a name
At once their country's glory and her shame!

— Frederick West, *The Story of Some Famous Books*

A Melancholy Author

The first edition of Robert Burton's *Anatomy of Melancholy* was published in 1621. The author is said to have composed it with a view to relieving his own melancholy, but increased it to such a degree, that nothing could make him laugh, but going to the bridgefoot and hearing the ribaldry of the bargemen, which rarely failed to throw him into a violent fit of laughter. Before he was overcome with this horrid disorder, he, in the intervals of his vapours, was esteemed one of the most facetious companions in the university. At Christ's Church College, where he died in 1640, at or very near the time he had some years before foretold from the calculation of his own nativity, several of the students did not forbear to whisper among themselves, that rather than there should be a mistake in the calculation, he sent up his soul to heaven through a slip about his neck.

— William Keddie, *Anecdotes Literary and Scientific*

A Critical Wife

When Robert Ainsworth (died 1743) was engaged in the laborious work of his Dictionary of the Latin language, his wife made heavy complaints at enjoying so little of his society. When he had reached the letter S of his work, the patience of his help-meet was completely exhausted; and, in a fit of ill-nature, she revenged herself for the loss of his company, by committing the whole manuscript to the flames! Such an accident would have deterred most men from prosecuting the undertaking; but the persevering industry of Ainsworth repaired the loss of his manuscript by the most assiduous application.

— William Keddie, *Anecdotes Literary and Scientific*

Isaac Newton's Other Accident

"What I heard today I must relate. There is one Mr. Newton (whom I have very often seen), Fellow of Trinity College, that is mighty famous for his learning, being a most excellent mathematician, philosopher, divine, etc. . . . Of all the books he ever wrote there was one of colours and light, established upon thousands of experiments, which he had been twenty years making, and which had cost him many hundreds of pounds. This book, which he valued so much, and which was so much talked of, had the ill-luck to perish and be utterly lost, just when the learned author was almost at pushing a conclusion to the same, after this manner: In a winter's morning, leaving it among his other papers on his study table, whilst he went to chapel, the candle, which he had unfortunately left burning there too, catched hold by some means of other papers, and they fired the aforesaid book, and utterly consumed it and several other valuable writings, and, which is most wonderful, did no further mischief. But when Mr. Newton came from chapel, and had seen what was done, every one thought he would have run mad; he was so troubled thereat that he was not himself for a month after."

— De la Pryme's Diary, February 3, 1692

I've had it with these cheap sons of bitches who claim they love poetry but never buy a book.

— Kenneth Rexroth

A Pox on Vulcan

(Written by Jonson after some of his manuscripts were destroyed by fire)

But to confine him to the Brew-houses,
The Glass-house, Dye-vats, and their Furnaces;
To live in Sea-coal, and go forth in Smoke;
Or lest that Vapour might the City choke
Condemn him to the Brick-kills, or some Hill —
Foot (out in Sussex) to an Iron Mill;
Or in small Fagots have him blaze about
Vile Taverns, and the Drunkards piss him out;
Or in the Bell-Man's Lanthorn like a Spy,
Burn to a Snuff, and then stink out and die,
Pox on your Flameship, Vulcan, if it be
To all as fatal as't hath been to me.

— Ben Jonson, *An Execration Upon Vulcan* (1691)

As for you, little envious Prigs, snarling, bastard, puny Criticks, you'll soon have railed your last: Go hang yourselves.
— François Rabelais (1492-1553)

A Critic Buries a Book and its Author

(Written on the death of William Chillingworth, January 30, 1644, author of *The Religion of Protestants: A Safe Way To Salvation*)

I shall undertake to bury his errours, which are published in this so much admired, yet unworthy booke; and happy would it be for this Kingdome, if this booke and all its fellows could be so buried, that they might never rise more, unless it were to a confutation. . . . Get thee gone then, thou cursed booke, which hath seduced so many precious soules; get thee gone, thou corrupt, rotten booke, earth to earth, and dust to dust; get thee gone into the place of rottennesse, that thou maiest rot with thy Author, and see corruption.

— Francis Cheynell, *The Sickness, Heresy, Death and Burial of William Chillingworth . . . and a Short Oration at the Buriall of his Hereticall Book*

Deadly Criticism?

The poet John Keats had something in common with Byron and Shelley: a small head. He developed all of his five senses to a high degree and once covered his tongue with cayenne pepper in order that he might better appreciate a cold draught of claret after it. All his life he sorrowed that he had done nothing worthy of abiding fame — once saying "Let my epitaph be: here lies one whose name was writ on water." His last words when he died in 1821, at the age of twenty-five, were: "Thank God it has come."

One school of thought suggests that, although he died of consumption, bad reviews in the *Quarterly Review* contributed to Keats' early demise. Byron referred to this in *Don Juan*:

"Poor fellow! His was an untoward fate; 'Tis strange the mind, that very fiery particle, should let itself be snuffed out by an article."

Poor Lamb!

Charles Lamb I sincerely believe to be in some considerable degree insane. A more pitiful, ricketty, gasping, staggering, stammering Tom-fool I do not know. . . . Besides, he is now a confirmed, shameless drunkard; asks vehemently for gin and water in strangers' houses; tipples till he is utterly mad, and is only not thrown out of doors because he is too much despised for taking such trouble with him. Poor Lamb! Poor England, when such a despicable abortion is named genius!

— Thomas Carlyle (1795–1881)

A Hack Writer's Epitaph

Here lies poor Ned Purdon, from misery freed,
Who long was a bookseller's hack;
He led such a damnable life in this world,
I don't think he'll ever come back.

— Oliver Goldsmith (1730–74)

Critical Spit

"What is a modern Poet's fate?
To write his thoughts upon a slate.
The critic spits on what is done, —
Gives it a wipe, and all is gone."

—Thomas Hood, *Whims and Oddities* (1827)

John Keats

Lord Byron

An Author's Rejection

Dr. Syntax:
"My errand was to bid you look
With care and candour on this book;
And tell me whether you think fit
To buy, or print, or publish it?"

The Bookseller:
"A Tour, indeed! — I've had enough
Of Tours, and such-like flimsy stuff.
What a fool's errand you have made
(I speak the language of the trade),
To travel all the country o'er,
And write what has been writ before!
We can get Tours — don't make wry faces,
From those who never saw the places.
I know a man who has the skill
To make your books of Tours at will;
And from his garret in Moorfields
Can see what ev'ry country yields;
So, if you please, you may retire,
And throw your book into the fire:
You need not grin, my friend, nor vapour;
I would not buy it for waste paper!"

— William Combe, *The Tour of Dr. Syntax in Search of the Picturesque* (1812)

There is probably no hell for authors in the next world — they suffer so much from critics and publishers in this.
— Christian Nestell Bovee (1820-1904)

A Witless Author

Whose chance it was to write this wretched book,
In the satiric mirror ne'er did look,
Wherein the witless author plain might see
Himself, from every spark of genius free.

— found in a translation of Martial's *Epigrams* (London, 1695)

A Poetic Fool

Sir, I admit your general rule,
That every poet is a fool,
But you yourself may serve to show it,
That every fool is not a poet.

— Alexander Pope (1688–1744)

Dr. Syntax and The Bookseller, illustrated by Thomas Rowlandson, 1812.

The life of writing men has always been . . . a bitter business. It is notoriously accompanied, for those who write well, by poverty and contempt; or by fatuity and wealth for those who write ill.

— Hilaire Belloc (1870-1953)

An Author Eats His Words, Literally

Authors have often been compelled to eat their words, but the operation has seldom been performed literally. In the seventeenth century, owing to the disastrous part which Christian IV of Denmark took in the Thirty Years' War, his kingdom was shorn of its ancient power and was overshadowed by the might of Sweden. One Theodore Reinking, lamenting the diminished glory of his race, wrote a book entitled *Dania ad exteros de perfidia Suecorum* (1644). It was not a very excellent work, neither was its author a learned or accurate historian, but it aroused the anger of the Swedes, who cast Reinking into prison. There he remained many years, when at length he was offered his freedom on the condition that he should either lose his head or eat his book. Our author preferred the latter alternative, and with admirable cleverness devoured his book when he had converted it into a sauce.

— P.H. Ditchfield, *Books Fatal to Their Authors*

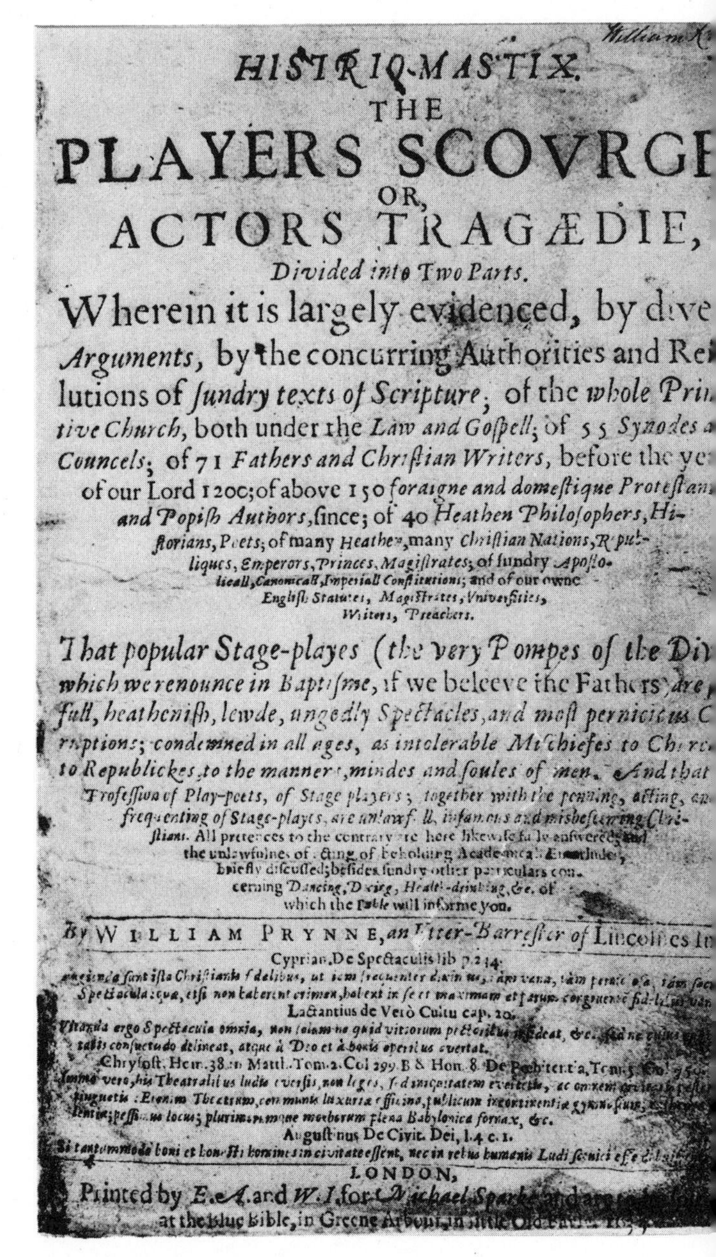
HISTRIO-MASTIX.
THE
PLAYERS SCOVRGE
OR,
ACTORS TRAGÆDIE,
Divided into Two Parts.
Wherein it is largely evidenced, by divers *Arguments*, by the concurring Authorities and Resolutions of *sundry texts of Scripture*; of the *whole Primitive Church*, both under the *Law and Gospell*; of 55 *Synodes and Councels*; of 71 *Fathers and Christian Writers*, before the yeare of our Lord 1200; of above 150 *forraigne and domestique Protestant and Popish Authors*, since; of 40 *Heathen Philosophers, Historians, Poets*; of many *Heathen*, many *Christian Nations, Republiques, Emperors, Princes, Magistrates*; of sundry *Apostolicall, Canonicall, Imperiall Constitutions*; and of our owne *English Statutes, Magistrates, Universities, Writers, Preachers.*

That popular Stage-playes (the very Pompes of the Divell which we renounce in Baptisme, if we beleeve the Fathers) *are sinfull, heathenish, lewde, ungodly Spectacles, and most pernicious Corruptions; condemned in all ages, as intolerable Mischiefes to Churches, to Republickes, to the manners, mindes and soules of men. And that the Profession of Play-poets, of Stage-players; together with the penning, acting, and frequenting of Stage-playes, are unlawfull, infamous and misbeseeming Christians.* All pretences to the contrary are here likewise fully answered; and the unlawfulnes of acting, of beholding Academicall Enterludes, briefly discussed; besides sundry other particulars concerning *Dancing, Dicing, Health-drinking, &c.* of which the *Table* will informe you.

By WILLIAM PRYNNE, *an Utter-Barrester of* Lincolnes Inne.

Cyprian. De Spectaculis lib. p. 2. 14.

Lactantius de Vero Cultu cap. 20.

Chrysost. Hom. 38. in Matth. Tom. 2. Col 299. B & Hom. 8. De Poenitentia, Tom. 5.

Augustinus De Civit. Dei, l. 4. c. 1.

LONDON,
Printed by E. A. and W. I. for Michael Sparke, and are to be sold at the blue Bible, in Greene Arbour, in little Old Baily.

The title page of William Prynne's disastrous book.

An Author Maimed

Maiming an author, cutting off his hands, or ears, or nose, seems to have been a favourite method of criticism in the sixteenth century. One John Stubbs had his right hand cut off for protesting against the proposed marriage of Queen Elizabeth with the Duke of Anjou, which bold act he committed to his work entitled *Discoveries of a Gaping Gulf whereinto England is like to be swallowed by another French marriage, if the Lord forbid not the banes by letting her Majestie see the sin and punishment thereof* (1579). Some believed that the book was far from being a libel on the Virgin Queen, but that it was written with great affection. However, it was pronounced to be "a fardell of false reports, suggestions, and manifest lies." Its author and Page, the bookseller, were brought into the open market at Westminster, and their right hands were cut off with a butcher's knife and mallet. With amazing loyalty, Stubbs took off his cap with his left hand and shouted, "Long live Queen Elizabeth!"

— P.H. Ditchfield, *Books Fatal to Their Authors*

There's nothing to writing. All you do is sit down at the typewriter and open a vein.
— Red Smith

The Awful Punishments of William Prynne

William Prynne, a barrister at Lincoln's Inn in London, published his *Histriomastix* — *The Player's Scourge*, in 1633, over which he had labored for seven years. In its 1100 closely printed pages he argued that stage-plays were "sinful, heathenish, intolerable mischiefs to churches, to republics, to the manners, minds and souls of men."

Contemporary feeling was that "neither the hospitality of the gentry in the time of Christmas, nor the music in cathedrals and the chapels royal, nor the pomps and gallantries of the Court, nor the Queen's harmless recreations, nor the King's (Charles I) solacing himself sometimes in masques and dances escaped the venom of his pen." He seemed to breathe nothing but disgrace to the nation, infamy to the Church, reproaches to the Court, dishonor to the Queen. (His remarks against female actors were thought to be aimed at Queen Henrietta Maria.)

The book and author were tried before the Star Chamber in Parliament and Laud, the Archbishop of Canterbury, passed sentence:

"I do in the first place begin censure with this book. I condemn it to be burnt in the most public manner that can be. The manner in other countries is (where such books are) to be burnt by the hangman, though not used in England (yet I wish it may, in respect of the strangeness and heinousness of the matter contained in it) to have a strange manner of burning; therefore I shall desire it may be burnt by the hand of the hangman. If it may agree with the Court, I do adjudge Mr. Prynne to be put from the Bar, to be forever uncapable of his profession. I do adjudge him, my Lords, that the Society of Lincoln's Inn do put him out of the Society; and because he had his offspring from Oxford" (now with a low voice said the Archbishop of Canterbury, "I am sorry that ever Oxford bred such an evil member") "there to be degraded. And I do condemn Mr. Prynne to stand in the pillory in two places, in Westminster and Cheapside, and that he shall lose both his ears, one in each place; and with a paper on his head declaring how foul an offence it is, viz. that it is for an infamous libel against both their Majesties, State and Government. And lastly (nay, not lastly) I do condemn him in £5,000 fine to the King. And lastly, perpetual imprisonment."

While in prison Prynne whiled away his time by writing further inflammatory books, among them *News From Ipswich* in 1637, which caused him to appear again before the Star Chamber.

During his second trial Sir J. Finch, Chief Justice of the Common Pleas, remarked: "I had thought Mr. Prynne had had no ears, but methinks he hath ears." Thereupon many Lords looked more closely at him, and the usher of the court was ordered to turn up his hair and show his ears. Their Lordships were displeased that no more had been cut off on the previous occasion.

The second punishment of William Prynne corrected this situation when he was condemned to be fined another £5,000, to be deprived of the remainder of his ears in the pillory, to be branded on both cheeks with "S.L." (Schismatical Libeller), and to be imprisoned for life in Carnarvon Castle.

"Come friend, come, burn me! Cut me! I fear not!" said Prynne to his executioner. "I have learned to fear the fire of hell, and not what man can do unto me. Come, scar me! Scar me!" The executioner proceeded to do this, with extraordinary severity, cruelly heating his iron twice, and cutting one of Prynne's ears so close as to take away a piece of the cheek. The mutilated author stirred not during the torture. When it was done, he smiled and observed: "The more I am beaten down, the more I am lifted up."

On his way back to prison he composed a verse on the two letters "S.L." branded on his cheek. Instead of "Schismatical Libeller", Prynne chose to call them "Stigmatus Laudis", the stigmas of his enemy the Archbishop Laud. Translated from his Latin it reads:

Bearing Laud's stamps on my cheek I retire
Triumphing, God's sweet sacrifice by fire.

Books are fatal: they are the curse of the human race.
— Benjamin Disraeli (1804-1881)

A Fatal Hoard of Books

For years, Eleanor Barry of Long Island, New York, had collected and hoarded books, newspapers, and magazines. In December of 1977, police were called to the seventy-year-old lady's house by worried neighbors who hadn't seen her for some time. On entering the house they found it filled to overflowing with towers of books from floor to ceiling. The policemen were forced to break down the bedroom door with an axe because a collapsed pile of books barred their way. Hearing faint cries for help they finally located Miss Barry who had been trapped beneath the enormous weight of fallen books while lying in her bed. Unfortunately she died shortly after being taken to hospital.

A Writer's Research Robbery

In July of 1978, a bank robber named Jack Drummond was shot and killed after drawing a gun on police during a hold up attempt in Columbus, Ohio. Further investigation revealed that he was a struggling New York mystery writer who had decided to attempt the robbery as research for his next book. His unfinished manuscript revealed that Drummond, who wrote under the name of George Redder, had written of the possibility of his own demise while attempting the robbery.

Authors Burn Better than Books

Books are not good fuel. . . . In the days when heretical books were burned, it was necessary to place them on large wooden stages, and after all the pains taken to demolish them, considerable readable masses were sometimes found in

Books and their authors being burned, from the Book of Martyrs *by John Foxe, 1563.*

the embers; whence it was supposed that the devil, conversant in fire and its effects, gave them his special protection. In the end it was found easier and cheaper to burn the heretics themselves than their books.

— J.H. Burton, *The Book Hunter*

William Tyndale at the Stake

Translators of the Bible fared not well at the hands of those who were unwilling that the Scriptures should be studied in the vulgar tongue by the layfolk, and foremost among that brave band of self-sacrificing scholars stands William Tyndale. After difficulties in attempting a translation of the New Testament in his native England, the Protestant Tyndale finally succeeded in doing so in 1526 in Belgium. It was immediately denounced by the Catholics, especially in England. However it was his work called *The Practice of Prelates*, mainly directed against the corruptions of the hierarchy and unfortunately containing a vehement condemnation of the divorce of Catherine of Arragon by Henry VIII, which was his final undoing. From this time on he was a wanted man. Henry Phillips, a Catholic in disguise, befriended Tyndale and lured him outside a "safe" house in Antwerp where he was captured and imprisoned in the Castle of Vilvoord. Here he petitioned for some warm clothing and "for a candle in the evening, for it is wearisome to sit alone in the dark," and above all for his Hebrew Bible, Grammar, and Dictionary, that he might spend his time in that study.

After a long dreary mockery of a trial on October 16, 1536, he was chained to a stake with faggots piled around him. As he stood firmly among the wood, with the executioner ready to strangle him, he lifted up his eyes to heaven and cried with a fervent zeal and loud voice, "Lord, open the King of England's eyes!" and then, yielding himself to the executioner, he was strangled, and his body immediately consumed.

— P.H. Ditchfield, *Books Fatal to Their Authors*

Some books are drenchèd sands
On which a great soul's wealth lies all in heaps,
Liked a wrecked argosy.
— Alexander Smith (1830-1867)

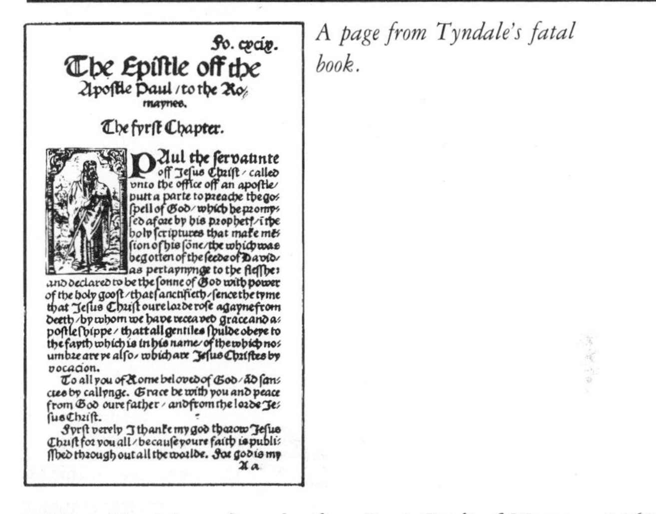

Fo. cxcix.

The Epistle off the Apostle Paul / to the Romaynes.

The fyrst Chapter.

Paul the servaunte off Jesus Christ / called unto the office off an apostle / putt a parte to preache the gospell of God / which he promysed afore by his prophetf / i the holy scriptures that make mension of his sone / the which was begotten of the seede of David / as pertaynynge to the flesshe: and declared to be the sonne of God with power of the holy goost / that sanctifieth / sence the tyme that Jesus Christ oure lorde rose agayne from deeth / by whom we have receaved grace and apostleshippe / thatt all gentiles shulde obeye to the fayth which is in his name / of the which noumbre are ye also / which are Jesus Christes by vocacion.

To all you of Rome beloved of God / ad sanctes by callynge. Grace be with you and peace from God oure father / and from the lorde Jesus Christ.

Fyrst verely I thanke my god thorow Jesus Christ for you all / because youre faith is publisshed through out all the worlde. For god is my

A a

A page from Tyndale's fatal book.

William Tyndale at the stake, from Foxe's Book of Martyrs, *1563.*

"Trial By Fire" by Pedro Berruguette, circa 1500. (Museo Del Prado, Madrid.)

CHAPTER FIVE

The Enemies of Books

The ravages of bookworms, books in flames,
the complaint of books against war, mutilated and battered books,
some current book troubles, banned books, and the destructive effects of dust,
water, neglect, and children.

It was a book to kill time for those who like it better dead.
— Rose MacAulay (1889-1958)

Good Luck, Little Book

Make haste away, and let one be
A friendly patron unto thee;
Lest, rapt from hence, I see thee lie
Torn for the use of pastery;
Or see thy injured leaves serve well
To make loose gowns for mackerel;
Or see the grocers, in a trice,
Make hoods of thee to serve out spice.

— Robert Herrick (1591–1674)

Treasures in the Toilet

In the summer of 1877, a gentleman with whom I was well acquainted took lodgings in Preston Street, Brighton. The morning after his arrival, he found in the toilet some leaves of an old black-letter (Gothic type) book. He asked permission to retain them, and enquired if there were any more where they came from. Two or three other fragments were found, and the landlady stated that her father, who was fond of antiquities, had at one time a chest full of old black-letter books; that, upon his death, they were preserved till she was tired of seeing them, and then, supposing them of no value, she had used them for waste; that for two years and a-half they had served for various household purposes, including toilet paper, but she had just come to the end of them. The fragments preserved, and now in my possession, are a goodly portion of one of the most rare books from the press of Wynkyn de Worde, Caxton's successor. The title is a curious woodcut with the words "Gesta Romanorum" engraved in an odd-shaped black letter. It has also numerous rude woodcuts throughout. It was from this very work that Shakespeare in all probability derived the story of the three caskets in which "The Merchant of Venice" forms so integral a portion of the plot. Only think of that sewer being supplied daily with such dainty bibliographical treasures!

— William Blades, *The Enemies of Books*

John Bagford, shoemaker and book-destroyer.

A Biblioclast

The memory of John Bagford (1675–1716), an antiquarian shoemaker, is held in deserved execration by bibliophiles. When the name of John Bagford is mentioned, book lovers hiss through their teeth, "Biblioclast!" and in that lies the secret of his misdoing. He spent his life in collecting materials for a history of printing which he never wrote. His materials were title-pages which he tore out and mounted with others in a book. It is said he collected about twenty-five thousand title-pages in all. His collection in sixty folio volumes, is deposited in the British Museum, a melancholy yet, professionally, an interesting collection. It is said that the closing hours of this arch-mutilator were embittered because he had been unable to discover and destroy a Caxton; but this was only because title-pages were unknown in England in Caxton's day.

— William S. Walsh, *A Handy-Book of Literary Curiosities*

The Abuse of Books in Bed

Richard Porson was a veritable slave to the habit of reading in bed during his tenure as professor of Greek at Cambridge. He would lie down with his books piled around him, then light his pipe and start in upon some favorite volume. A jug of liquor was invariably at hand, for Porson was a famous drinker. On one occasion he fell into a boozy slumber, his pipe dropped out of his mouth and set fire to the bedclothes. But for the arrival of succor the tipsy scholar and his books would surely have been cremated.

Another very slovenly fellow devoted to reading in bed was Thomas De Quincey. Thus reclined, De Quincey was a very vandal when it came to the care and use of books. He never returned volumes he borrowed, and he never hesitated to mutilate a rare book in order to save himself the labor and trouble of writing out a quotation.

— Eugene Field, *The Love Affairs of a Bibliomaniac*

The Complaint of Books Against War

Does it afflict you to find your books wearing out? I mean literally. . . . The mortality of all inanimate things is terrible to me, but that of books most of all.
— William Dean Howells (1837-1920)

Almighty Author and Lover of Peace, scatter the nations that seek after war, which harms books beyond all pestilences. For wars, which lack a ground in reason, make furious assaults upon all that is opposed to them and, discarding the governance of reason, proceed without discreet judgment and destroy the vessels of reason.

Truly, we have not sufficiency to make worthy lament for the separate books which have perished in various parts of the world by the perils of war. Yet we select for mournful mention that awful slaughter which happened in Egypt in the first Alexandrian war under the auxiliaries. There in the flames perished the seventy thousand volumes which were collected through many generations of time under the Ptolemies, as Aulus Gellius recites in the sixteenth chapter of the sixth book of his *Noctes Atticae*. How great a progeny of Atlas may be thought to have perished at that time! — the motions of the orbits, all the conjunctions of the planets, the nature of the Milky Way, and the prognostic generations of the comets, and whatsoever things happened in the heavens or are comprehended in the ether. Who would not shudder at so unholy a burnt offering, where ink is offered up in place of blood, where the glowing ashes of crackling parchment were dyed red with blood, where the devouring flame consumed so many thousands of innocents in whose mouths guile was not found, and where the unsparing fire turned into foul ashes so many receptacles of eternal truth!

Think ye the apodictic syllogism regarding the squaring of the circle would have escaped Aristotle in the least, if shameful wars had permitted the books of the ancients, which contained the laws of all nature, to survive? Neither would he have set forth the problem of the eternity of the world as indeterminate; nor, as is believed with plausibility, would he have doubted in any wise of the plurality of human intellects and of their eternity, if the perfect sciences of the ancients had not been exposed to the destruction of hateful wars. For by wars are we dragged away to foreign lands, are killed and wounded and frightfully disfigured, are buried beneath the earth, drowned in the sea, burned in the fire, and slain by every kind of death. How much of our blood was shed by the warlike Scipio, when he eagerly set himself to the overthrowing of Carthage, the opposer and rival of the Roman power! What thousands of thousands the

ten years' Trojan war sent out of the light! How many, when Tully was slain, were sent by Antony to seek hiding places in foreign provinces! How many of us, at the exile of Boethius, were scattered by Theodoric in divers regions of the world, like sheep whose shepherd had been smitten! How many, when Seneca fell before the malice of Nero, and willing yet unwilling, approached the gates of death, were parted from him and withdrew weeping, wholly unknowing in what parts we could seek refuge!

But endless are the losses inflicted on the race of books by the tumults of war; and as it is in no wise possible to survey all the infinite, here let us finally establish the Gades of our complaint and draw rein in our course, turning to the prayers with which we began, humbly asking that the Ruler of Olympus and the Most High Dispenser of all things may insure peace, remove wars, and make the times tranquil under His own protection.

— Richard de Bury, *The Philobiblon* (1345)

I tear old writings bit by bit,
And what care I for bookish forms;
Dead men are drier than their wit —
Both wit and bones are food for worms!

— *The Bookworm*

The Bookworms

(Burns saw a splendidly bound but sadly neglected copy of Shakespeare in the library of a nobleman in Edinburgh, and he wrote these lines on the ample margin of one of its pages, where they were found long after the poet's death.)

Through and through the inspired leaves,
Ye maggots, make your windings;
But oh, respect his lordship's taste,
And spare the golden bindings.

— Robert Burns (1759–1796)

Yet, why should sons of science
These puny rankling reptiles dread?
'Tis but to let their books be read,
And bid the worms defiance.
— J. Doraston, 1888

Hunting the Bookworm

Come hither, boy, we'll hunt to-day
The bookworm, ravening beast of prey,
Produc'd by parent Earth, at odds,
As fame reports it, with the gods.
Him frantic hunger wildly drives
Against a thousand authors' lives:
Through all the fields of wit he flies;
Dreadful his head with clustering eyes,
With horns without, and tusks within,
And scales to serve him for a skin.
Observe him nearly, lest he climb
To wound the bards of ancient time,
Or down the vale of fancy go
To tear some modern wretch below.
On every corner fix thine eye,
Or ten to one he slips thee by.

See where his teeth a passage eat:
We'll rouse him from his deep retreat.
But who the shelter's forc'd to give?
'T is sacred Virgil, as I live!
From leaf to leaf, from song to song
He draws the tadpole form along,
He mounts the gilded edge before,
He's up, he scuds the cover o'er,
He turns, he doubles, there he past,
And here we have him, caught at last.

— Theodore Beza (1519–1605), translated from Latin by Thomas Parnell (1679–1718).

The Bookworm, magnified eleven times, from Micrographia *by Robert Hooke, 1665.*

The Beautiful California Bookworm

Examined microscopically this small worm was found to be not only interesting, but in some degree even beautiful.

I first weighed my little captive on a delicate balance and found him to turn the beam at three and four-tenths milligrammes. I found his extreme length when extended in creeping to be eight millimetres; on being intercepted he contracted to five; his extreme thickness while in motion was about one millimetre. In one minute he advanced nine centimetres.

My optical study showed him to be a series of joints, thirteen or fourteen in number; all of these were silver white, translucent in some lights and transparent in others; they were composed of minute shining scales. The whole body was flattened cylindrical and tapered regularly toward the tail. On some parts of the body were seen hairs, thinly distributed, without seeming regularity or purpose. The head was amber colored, flattened, and marked with two divisions. Projecting from the head in front, might be seen two short antennae, which slipped into a sleeve or sheath when the animal was alarmed. The two prominent eyes seemed to be composite, but I could not be sure of this; and he was provided with two cutting instruments resembling those of the teredo navalis; there were ten sucker-like feet and six arms, the latter each terminating in a claw of dark color.

When properly lighted, the animal was so nearly transparent that the viscera could be distinctly seen, and their action clearly observed and studied; red blood with floating corpuscles was in visible circulation; the pulsations of the heart or lungs were twenty-six per minute.

— Henry G. Banks at a meeting of the San Francisco Microscopical Society, June 16, 1897.

What is written is merely the dregs of experience.
— Franz Kafka (1883-1924)

A Lady Burns Her Husband's Manuscript

Lady Burton was the widow of Sir Richard Burton, the translator of the unexpurgated *Arabian Nights*, which raised a howl of indignation among strait-laced moralists. On the completion of that work he gave himself up entirely to translating *The Scented Garden*. It treated of a certain passion. The day before his sudden and unexpected death he called Lady Burton into his room, and told her that the work was now all but completed, and that he purposed to set apart the proceeds as an annuity for her. Next day he was no more. When she came to look over his manuscripts she for the first time fully understood the nature of *The Scented Garden*. A publisher had offered her six thousand pounds for it. For three days she was in a state of torture. Finally she decided to destroy it:

"I sat down on the floor before the fire at dark to consult my own heart, my own head. My head told me that sin is the only rolling stone that gathers moss; that what a gentleman, a scholar, a man of the world may write when living, he would see very differently to what the poor soul would see standing naked before its God, with its good or evil deeds alone to answer for, and their consequences visible to it for the first moment, rolling on to the end of time. I fetched the manuscript and laid it on the ground before me, — two large volumes' worth. Still my thoughts were, Was it a sacrilege? It was his *magnum opus*, — his last work, that he was so proud of, that was to have been finished on the awful morrow — that never came. Will he rise up in his grave and curse me or bless me? The thought will haunt me to death. And then I said, "Not only not for six thousand guineas, but not for six million guineas, will I risk it." Sorrowfully, reverently, and in fear and trembling, I burnt sheet after sheet until the whole of the volume was consumed."

— William S. Walsh, *A Handy-Book of Literary Curiosities*

Raging Raleigh Destroys the World

Sir Walter Raleigh's *History of the World* was composed during his imprisonment in the Tower of London. Only a small portion of the work was published, owing to the following singular circumstances: One afternoon looking through his window into one of the courts in the Tower, Sir Walter saw two men quarrel, when the one actually murdered the other; and shortly after two gentlemen, friends to Sir Walter, coming into his room, after expressing what had happened, they disagreed in their manner of relating the story; and Sir Walter, who had seen it himself, concurred that neither was accurate, but related it with another variation. The three eye-witnesses disagreeing about an act so recently committed put Sir Walter in a rage, when he took up the volumes of manuscript which lay by, containing his *History of the World*, and threw them on a large fire that was in the room, exclaiming that "it was not for him to write the history of the world, if he could not relate what he saw a quarter of an hour before." One of his friends saved two of the volumes from the flames, but the rest were consumed. The world laments that so strange an accident should have mutilated the work of so extraordinary a man.

— *Granger's Wonderful Magazine*

Books in Flames

There are many of the forces of Nature which tend to injure Books; but among them all not one has been half so destructive as Fire. It would be tedious to write out a bare list only of the numerous libraries and bibliographical treasures which, in one way or another, have been seized by the Fire-king as his own. Chance conflagrations, fanatic incendiarism, Judicial bonfires, and even household stoves have, time after time, thinned the treasures as well as the rubbish of past ages, until, probably, not one thousandth part of the books that have been are still extant. This destruction cannot, however, be reckoned as all loss; for had not the "cleansing fires" removed mountains of rubbish from our midst, strong destructive measures would become a necessity from sheer want of space in which to store so many volumes.

The Invention of Printing made the entire destruction of any author's works much more difficult, so quickly and so extensively did books spread through all lands. On the other hand, as books multiplied, so did destruction go hand in hand with production, and soon were printed books doomed to suffer in the same penal fires, that up to then had been fed on manuscripts only.

— William Blades, *The Enemies of Books*

We all know that books burn — yet we have the greater knowledge that books cannot be killed by fire. People die, but books never die. No man and no force can abolish memory. . . . In this war, we know, books are weapons.
— Franklin Delano Roosevelt (1882-1945)

Some Victims of Nazi Book Burnings

Books by Catholic, Jewish, Marxist and assorted "un-German" authors were favorites for the flames in pre-war Nazi Germany. Among the thousands of volumes consumed in public burnings (often conducted by the Minister of Public Enlightenment, Joseph Goebbels), were books by Sholem Asch, John Dos Passos, Albert Einstein, Sigmund Freud, Maxim Gorky, Ernest Hemingway, Helen Keller, V.I. Lenin, Jack London, Thomas Mann, Karl Marx, Marcel Proust, Erich Maria Remarque, Upton Sinclair, Joseph Stalin, Leon Trotsky, H.G. Wells, and Arnold Zweig.

There is no book so bad but there is something good in it.
— Miguel Cervantes (1547-1616)

An Indignant Remonstrance to an Arsonist

(The remonstrance is supposed to be addressed to a Communist, whose incendiary rage has just destroyed a Parisian library. After having been eloquently reproached for quenching the light of reason in his own soul, and destroying his own heritage, the Communist replies in this epigrammatic ending so characteristic of Victor Hugo, and so crushingly unanswerable: "I cannot read.")

'Tis you then burned the library?

I did, I brought the fire.

— O most unheard-of crime,
Crime, wretch, which you upon yourself commit!
Why, you have quenched the light of your own soul!
'Tis your own torch which you have just put out!
That which your impious madness has dared burn,
Was your own treasure, fortune, heritage!
The Book (the master's bugbear) is your gain!
The Book has ever taken side with you.
A Library implies an act of faith
Which generations still in darkness hid
Sign in their night in witness of the dawn.
What! miscreant, you fling your flaming torch
Into this pile of venerable truths,
These master-works that thunder forth and lighten,
Into this tomb become time's inventory,
Into the ages, the antique man, the past
Which still spells out the future — history
Which having once begun will never end,
Into the poets! Into this mine of Bibles
And all this heap divine — dread Aeschylus,
Homer, and Job upright against th' horizon,
Molière, Voltaire and Kant you set on fire!
Thus turning human reason into smoke!
Have you forgotten that your liberator
Is this same Book? The Book that's set on high
And shines; because it lightens and illumes;

I see no point in reading.
— Louis XIV (1638-1715)

It undermines the gallows, war and famine;
It speaks; the Slave and Pariah disappear.
Open a Book. Plato, Beccaria, Milton,
Those prophets, Dante, Shakespeare or Corneille,
Shall not their great souls waken yours in you?
Dazzled you feel the same as each of them;
Reading you grow more gentle, pensive, grave;
Within your heart you feel these great men grow;
They teach you as the dawn lights up a cloister,
And as their warm beams penetrate your heart
You are appeased and thrill with stronger life;
Your soul interrogated answers theirs;
You feel you're good, then better; — as snow in fire —
Then melt away your pride, your prejudice,
Evil and rage and Kings and Emperors!
For Science, you see, first lays hold of men,
Then Liberty, and all this flood of light,
Mark me, 'tis you who have extinguished it!
The goal you dreamt of by the Book was reached;
The Book enters your thoughts and there unties
The bonds wherein truth was by error held,
For each man's conscience is a Gordian knot.
The Book is your physician, guardian, guide:
It heals your hate, and cures your frenzied mood.
See what you lose by your own fault, alas!
Why, know the Book's your wealth! The Book means truth,
Knowledge and Duty, Virtue, Progress, Right,
And Reason scattering hence delirious dreams.
And you destroy this, you!

I cannot read.

— Victor Hugo (1802–1885),
L'Année Terrible

Books being rescued from a burning library.

Victor Hugo.

I hate books; they only teach us to talk about things we know nothing about.

— Jean-Jacques Rousseau (1712-1778)

A Short List of Banned Books

Analects (the sayings of Confucius, 551–478 B.C., and his disciples) was burnt and hundreds of the disciples burnt alive by the first ruler of the Ts'in dynasty in 250 B.C., who wished to abolish the feudal system. Thirty years later the emperor Chi Huang Ti burned all those copies that had survived the earlier purge in an attempt to disprove the traditional Chinese culture.

Confucius, the first banned author.

The Emperor burning the books of Confucius.

You despise books; you, whose whole lives are absorbed in the vanities of ambition, the pursuit of pleasure or in indolence; but remember that all the known world, excepting only savage nations, is governed by Books.
— Voltaire (1694-1778)

Llysistrata (Aristophanes, 411 B.C.) was pronounced obscene by Plutarch in 66 B.C. and banned in the United States until 1930 for the same reason.

Ars Amatoria (Ovid, 1 B.C.) was banned in Rome in 8 A.D. and Ovid banished to Greece. In 1497 the book, along with the works of Dante, was deemed erotic, impious, and corrupting and burnt in a huge bonfire in Rome. In 1928 *Ars Amatoria* was barred by United States customs and banned in San Francisco in 1929.

Pro Populo Anglicano Defensio (John Milton, 1651) was burned in France for political reasons in 1652 and in England in 1660 because it attacked the king, Charles I. (The author barely escaped the same fate as his book.)

The Scarlet Letter (Nathaniel Hawthorne, 1850) was banned in Russia from 1852 to 1856 and condemned in America in 1852 as perpetrating bad morals.

Wonder Stories (Hans Christian Andersen, 1835) was forbidden to readers in Russia from 1835 to 1849 and allowed to be read by adults only in the state of Illinois in 1954 so that young readers could not "obtain smut."

Leaves of Grass (Walt Whitman, 1855) was considered obscene on publication and only one library (in Philadelphia) bought the book. In 1882 it was banned in Boston but published again in Philadelphia.

The Kreutzer Sonata (Leo Tolstoy, 1889) was forbidden publication in Switzerland, England, and Germany and the United States. Teddy Roosevelt called the author "a sexual and moral pervert." It was banned in Russia in 1926 and in Italy in 1929.

The Adventures of Tom Sawyer (Mark Twain, 1876), along with *Huckleberry Finn,* was banned from the children's room of the public library in Brooklyn as bad examples for youth. Both books were banned in Russia from 1930 to 1946 and in 1957 were eliminated from the approved list of school books in New York.

Ulysses (James Joyce, 1922) was burned in its year of publication by the United States Post Office and by government agencies in Ireland and Canada. 499 copies were burned by British Customs in 1923 and 500 copies by the United States Post Office in the same year. It was formally banned in England in 1929 but finally allowed into the United States after a lengthy court battle, in 1933.

Get stewed: books are a load of crap.
— Philip Larkin

Some Current Book Troubles

Recent reports by the International Association of Poets, Playwrights, Editors, Essayists, and Novelists (PEN) and various news sources around the world show that authors and their books continue to suffer. The list of countries where authors have been chastised, harassed, or imprisoned and/or their books banned, censored, or condemned by governments or individuals includes: South Africa, Egypt, East Germany, West Germany, Hungary, Iran, Israel, Kenya, South Korea, The Philippines, Poland, Russia, the United States, and Yugoslavia.
Some specific incidents in 1979 included:

- South Africa — Government censors banned *Burger's Daughter* by South African author Nadine Gordimer because the book depicts "whites as baddies" and "blacks as goodies." Also banned were *A Dry White Season* by Andre Brink (because he didn't first submit it to the censors) and *Sophie's Choice* by William Styron.

- Egypt — On the grounds that the book was heretical and therefore unfit for public reading, the government banned the book of Muhyi al-Dinibn Arabi, an Islamic mystic who lived 800 years ago.

- West Germany — An antiquarian book dealer was prosecuted for buying two copies of a Nazi edition of *Mein Kampf* by Adolph Hitler. Eight books that "glorified the Nazi regime," including a book *The Fraud of the Century*, were banned by the government from public display.

- Israel — The censorship board, composed of senior cabinet members, prohibited the former prime minister Rabin from including in his memoirs an account of the expulsion of 50,000 Palestinians during the Arab-Israeli war of 1948.

- South Korea — Representations from many organizations failed to obtain the release of imprisoned dissident writers Kim Chi Ha and Yang Song Woo.

- United States — The American Library Association's Office for Intellectual Freedom reported 1979 as the worst year in the past twenty five for book persecution in America, with growing numbers of communities and school boards banning, censoring, or removing books from classrooms. Among these latter books were: *The American Heritage Dictionary*; *The Catcher in the Rye* by J.D. Salinger;

"Still Life" by Harmen Steenwyck (1612–1655).
(The National Gallery, London.)

Black Boy by Richard Wright, and all the works of Richard Brautigan.

❦ The only reported book burning in 1979 took place in February in Adrian, Michigan, where the Rev. Rick Strawcutter led a public burning of *The Man* by Irving Wallace.

There will always be a mob with a torch ready when someone cries, "Burn those books!"

— Henry Seidel Canby

Contemporary books do not keep. The quality in them which makes for their success is the first to go; they turn overnight.
— Cyril Connolly (1903-1974)

Water

Next to Fire we must rank Water in its two forms, liquid and vapour, as the greatest destroyer of books. Thousands of volumes have been actually drowned at sea, and no more heard of them than of the sailors to whose charge they were committed.

Mohammed II, upon the capture of Constantinople in the fifteenth century, after giving up the devoted city to be sacked by his licentious soldiers, ordered the books in all the churches as well as the great library of the Emperor Constantine, containing 120,000 manuscripts, to be thrown into the sea.

In the shape of rain, water has frequently caused irreparable injury. Positive wet is fortunately of rare occurrence in a library, but it is very destructive when it does come, and, if long continued, the substance of the paper succumbs to the unhealthy influence and rots and rots until all fibre disappears, and the paper is reduced to a white decay which crumbles into powder when handled.

Water in the form of vapour is a great enemy of books, the damp attacking both outside and inside. Outside it fosters the growth of a white mould or fungus which vegetates upon the edges of the leaves, upon the sides and in the joints of the binding. Inside the book, damp encourages the growth of those ugly brown spots which so often disfigure prints and 'livres de luxe.'

In a perfectly dry and warm library these spots would probably remain undeveloped. The fact is that books should never be allowed to get really cold, for when a thaw comes and the weather sets in warm, the air, laden with damp, penetrates the inmost recesses, and working its way between the volumes and even between the leaves, deposits upon their cold surface its moisture.

— William Blades, *The Enemies of Books*

Dust and Neglect

Dust upon Books to any extent points to neglect, and neglect means more or less slow Decay. A well-gilt top to a book is a great preventive against damage by dust, while to leave books with rough tops and unprotected is sure to produce stains and dirty margins.

Let us now enter the communal library of some large provincial town. The interior has a lamentable appearance; dust and disorder have made it their home. It has a librarian, but he has the consideration of a porter only, and goes but once a week to see the state of the books committed to his care; they are in a bad state, piled in heaps and perishing in corners for want of attention and binding. At this present time more than one public library in Paris could be mentioned in which thousands of books are received annually, all of which will have disappeared in the course of 50 years or so for want of binding; there are rare books, impossible to replace, falling to pieces because no care is given to them, that is to say, they are left unbound, a prey to dust and the worm, and cannot be touched without dismemberment.

— L. Derome, *Le Luxe des Livres*

Disintegrating Books

In March of 1980 it was discovered that many of the old books in the United States, particularly those published since 1850, were in very poor condition because of acid in the paper on which they were printed. Experts predicted that 97 percent of all books published between 1900 and 1937 have useful lives of fifty years or less remaining and that many of the books being printed today have a life expectancy of between thirty and fifty years. The New York Public Library estimated that fully one half of its five million books were so badly decayed that they were on the verge of disintegration.

An Abused Book's Lament

Your borrowers of books — *those mutilators of collections — spoilers of the symmetry of shelves, and creators of odd volumes.*
— Charles Lamb (1775-1834)

I'm a castaway fellow, all dingy and yellow,
Forsaken I lie on the dark garret floor;
All wretched and lonely, for now I am only
A mere wreck of what was a beauty before.

My pride is all shattered, my leaves they are battered,
And all of them cruelly scribbled and torn.
I have but one cover, they tore off the other —
And that one is dreadfully battered and worn.

An old-fashioned bonnet, a faded rose on it,
A rusty jack-knife, a shoe out at the toe,
A pile of old papers, three dirty wax tapers,
Are my only companions in these hours of woe.

Once I lived in a city, where books bright and pretty
Were ranged in a long shining row on the shelf.
I'd an exquisite cover, gilt-lettered all over,
And not one was more beautiful there than myself.

My next place of dwelling — I blush at the telling —
Was a schoolroom as dusty as dusty could be,
Where long I was studied, scratched, thumb-marked and muddied,
And ruined as any one plainly can see.

And here I am lying, degraded and dying,
While old dusty cobwebs are covering me o'er,
Alone and forsaken, while naught can awaken
The glory I knew in the sweet days of yore.

— Lillie Sheldon, in *Book-Song*

"Enemies of the Book", as drawn by Gustav Doré. (The Bettmann Archive, New York.)

CHAPTER SIX

The Love of Books

Books as intimate bedfellows, boon companions, faithful friends, sensual lovers, learned educators, and entertainers with eloquent thoughts on their diversions, immortality, passions, pleasures, powers, solace, truth, value, wit, and wisdom.

"A Lady Teaching A Child To Read" by Caspar Netscher (1635–1684). (The National Gallery, London.)

A good book is the best of friends, the same today and for ever.
— Martin Tupper (1810-1889)

The Perfect Friend

Oh! but books are such safe company! They keep your Secrets well; *they* never boast that they made your eyes glisten, or your cheek flush, or your heart throb. You may take up your favourite Author, and love him at a distance just as warmly as you like, for all the sweet fancies and glowing thoughts that have winged your lonely hours so fleetly and so sweetly. Then you may close the book, and lean your cheek against the cover, as if it were the face of a dear friend; shut your eyes and soliloquoise to your heart's content, without fear of misconstruction, even though you should exclaim in the fulness of your enthusiasm, "What an *adorable soul that man has*!" You may put the volume under your pillow, and let your eye and the first ray of morning light fall on it together, and nothing shall rob you of that delicious pleasure. You may have a thousand petty, provoking, irritating annoyances through the day, and you shall come back again to your dear old book, and forget them all in dreamland. It shall be a friend that shall be always at hand; that shall never try you by caprice, or pain you by forgetfulness, or wound you by distrust.

— Sara P. Parton (Fanny Fern: 1811–1872), *Fern Leaves*

Sensual Delight

How differently do mental pleasures
Lead us from book to book to roam
And ever, with these ancient treasures,
How cheerful winter nights become!

A happy life grows warm in every limb;
And if a precious parchment you unroll,
Your senses in delight appear to swim
And heaven itself descends upon your soul.

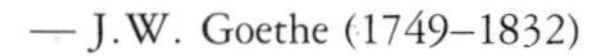

— J.W. Goethe (1749–1832)

Seized with Rapture

Golden volumes! richest treasures!
Objects of delicious pleasures!
You my eyes rejoicing please,
You my hands in rapture seize!
Brilliant wits, and musing sages,
Lights who beamed through many ages,
Left to your conscious leaves their story,
And dared to trust you with their glory;
And now their hope of fame achieved!
Dear volumes! you have not deceived!

— Isaac Disraeli (1767–1848)

Petrarch's Friends

I have FRIENDS, whose society is extremely agreeable to me: they are of all ages, and of every country. They have distinguished themselves both in the cabinet and in the field, and obtained high honors for their knowledge of the sciences. It is easy to gain access to them; for they are always at my service, and I admit them to my company, and dismiss them from it, whenever I please. They are never troublesome, but immediately answer every question I ask them. Some relate to me the events of past ages, while others reveal to me the secrets of nature. Some, by their vivacity, drive away my cares and exhilarate my spirits, while others give fortitude to my mind, and teach me the important lesson how to restrain my desires, and to depend wholly on myself. They open to me, in short, the various avenues of all the arts and sciences, and upon their information I safely rely, in all emergencies. In return for all these services, they only ask me to accommodate them with a convenient chamber in some corner of my humble habitation, where they may repose in peace: for these friends are more delighted by the tranquility of retirement, than with the tumults of society.

— Francesco Petrarca (1304–1374)

Come, and take a choice of all my library;
And so beguile thy sorrow.
— William Shakespeare (1564-1616)

Books Are the Windows of the Soul

Books are the windows through which the soul looks out. A home without books is like a room without windows. No man has the right to bring up his children without surrounding them with books, if he has the means to buy them. It is a wrong to his family. He cheats them! Children learn to read by being in the presence of books. The love of knowledge comes with reading and grows upon it. And the love of knowledge, in a young mind, is almost a warrant against the inferior excitement of passions and vices. Let us pity these poor rich men who live barrenly in great bookless houses! Let us congratulate the poor that, in our day, books are so cheap that a man may every year add a hundred volumes to his library for the price which his tobacco and his beer would cost him. Among the earliest ambitions to be excited in clerks, workmen, journeymen, and, indeed, among all that are struggling up in life from nothing to something, is that of forming and continually adding to a library of good books. A little library, growing larger every year, is an honourable part of a man's history. It is a man's duty to have books. A library is not a luxury, but one of the necessities of life.

— Henry Ward Beecher (1813-1887): *Sermons*

Books are hindrances to persisting stupidity.
— Spanish Proverb

A Passionate Love Affair with Books

Sitting last winter among my books, and walled round with all the comfort and protection which they and my fireside could afford me, — to wit, a table of high-piled books at my back, my writing desk on one side of me, some shelves on the other, and the feeling of the warm fire at my feet, — I began to consider how I loved the authors of those books; how I loved them too, not only for the imaginative pleasures they afforded me, but for their making me love the very books themselves, and delight to be in contact with them. I looked sideways at my Spenser, my Theocritus, and my Arabian Nights; then above them at my Italian Poets; then behind me at my Dryden and Pope, my Romances, and my Boccaccio; then on my left side at my Chaucer, who lay on my writing desk; and thought how natural it was in Charles Lamb to give a kiss to an old folio, as I once saw him do to Chapman's Homer. . . .

At all events, nothing, while I live and think, can deprive me of my value for such treasures. I can help the appreciation of them while I last, and love them till I die; and perhaps, if fortune turns her face once more in kindness upon me before I go, I may chance, some quiet day, to lay my over-beating temples on a book, and so have the death I most envy.

— Leigh Hunt, *My Books* (1823)

To an Old Book

Old book forlorn, compiled of ancient thought,
Now bought and sold, and once more sold and bought,
At last left stranded, where in time I spied,
Borne thither by an impecunious tide;
Well thumbed, stain-marked, but new and dear to me,
My purse and thy condition well agree.
I saw thee, yearned, then took thee to my arms,
For fellowship in misery has charms.
How long, I know not, thou hadst lain unscanned,
Thy mellow leaves untouched by loving hand —
For there thou wast beneath a dusty heap,
Unknown. I raised thee, therefore let me reap
A harvest from thy treasures. Thee I found —
Yea, thee I'll cherish; though new friends abound,
I'll still preserve thee as the years go round.

— Edgar Greenleaf Bradford, in *Book-Song*

A medieval Jewish Prayer Book. (The Victoria & Albert Museum, London.)

Philobiblon

(Written by Richard De Bury, 1287-1345)

In Books we find the dead as it were living; in Books we foresee things to come; in Books warlike affairs are methodized; the rights of peace proceed from Books. All things are corrupted and decay with time. Saturn never ceases to devour those whom he generates, insomuch that the glory of the world would be lost in oblivion if God had not provided mortals with a remedy in Books. Alexander the ruler of the world; Julius the invader of the world and of the city, and first who in unity of person assumed the empire in arms and arts; the faithful Fabricius, the rigid Cato, would at this day have been without a memorial if the aid of Books had failed them. Towers are razed to the earth, cities overthrown, triumphal arches mouldered to dust; nor can the King or Pope be found, upon whom the privilege of a lasting name can be conferred more easily than by Books.

Lastly, let us consider how great a commodity of doctrine exists in Books, how easily, how secretly, how safely they expose the nakedness of human ignorance without putting it to shame. These are the masters who instruct us without rods and ferules, without hard words and anger, without clothes or money. If you approach them, they are not asleep, if investigating you interrogate them, they conceal nothing; if you mistake them, they never grumble; if you are ignorant, they cannot laugh at you.

You only, O Books, are liberal and independent. You give to all who ask, and enfranchise all who serve you assiduously. Truly you are the ears filled with most palatable grains. You are golden urns in which manna is laid up, rocks flowing with honey, or rather indeed honeycombs; udders most copiously yielding the milk of life, storerooms ever full; the four-streamed river of Paradise, where the human mind is fed, and the arid intellect moistened and watered; fruitful olives, vines of Engaddi, fig-trees knowing no sterility; burning lamps to be ever held in the hand.

The library, therefore, of wisdom is more precious than all riches, and nothing that can be wished for is worthy to be compared with it. Whosoever, therefore, acknowledges himself to be a zealous follower of truth, of happiness, of wisdom, of science, or even of the faith, must of necessity make himself a Lover of Books.

— Translated from the Latin by J.B. Inglis (London 1832)

People say that life is the thing, but I prefer reading.
—Logan Pearsall Smith (1865-1946)

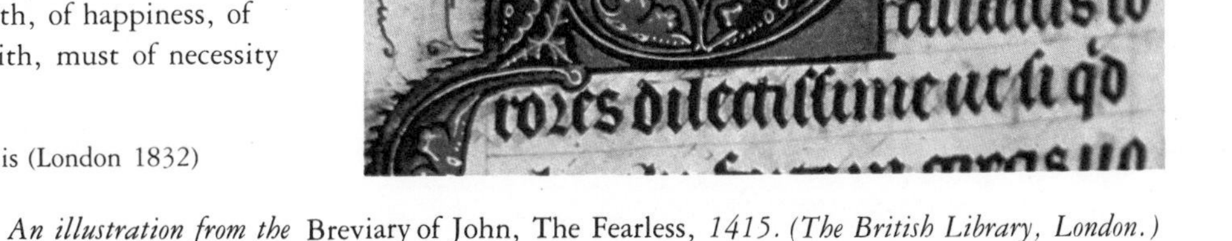

An illustration from the Breviary of John, The Fearless, *1415. (The British Library, London.)*

I have sought for happiness everywhere, but I have found it nowhere except in a little corner with a little book.
— Thomas à Kempis (1380-1471)

The Consolations of Literature

I find my joy and solace in literature. There is no gladness that this cannot increase; no sorrow that it cannot lessen. Troubled as I am by the ill health of my wife, by the dangerous condition — sometimes, alas! by death — of my friends, I fly to my studies as the one alleviation of my fears. They do me this service — they make me understand my troubles better, and bear them more patiently. . . . Certainly there is a pleasure in these pursuits, but they themselves prosper best when the mind is light.

— Pliny (23-79)

A Small, Old-Fashioned Book Works Miracles

At last Maggie's eyes glanced down on the books that lay on the window-shelf, and she half forsook her reverie to turn over listlessly the leaves of the "Portrait Gallery," but she soon pushed this aside to examine the little row of books tied together with string. "Beauties of the Spectator," "Rasselas," "Economy of Human Life," "Gregory's Letter" — she knew the sort of matter that was inside all these: the "Christian year" — that seemed to be a hymn book, and she laid it down again; but *Thomas à Kempis?* — the name had come across her in her reading, and she felt the satisfaction, which every one knows, of getting some ideas to attach to a name that strays solitary in the memory. She took up the little, old, clumsy book with some curiosity: it had the corners turned down in many places, and some hand, now for ever quiet, had made at certain passages strong pen and ink marks, long since browned by time.

She read on and on in the old book, devouring eagerly the dialogues with the invisible Teacher, the pattern of sorrow, the source of all strength; returning to it after she had been called away, and reading till the sun went down behind the willows. She knew nothing of doctrines and systems — of mysticism or quietism but this voice out of the far-off middle ages was the direct communication of a human soul's belief and experience, and came to Maggie as an unquestioned message.

I suppose that is the reason why the small old-fashioned book, for which you need only pay sixpence at a book-stall, works miracles to this day, turning bitter waters into sweetness: while expensive sermons and treatises, newly issued, leave all things as they were before. It was written down by a hand that waited for the heart's prompting; it is the chronicle of a solitary, hidden anguish, struggle, trust and triumph — not written on velvet cushions to teach endurance to those who are treading with bleeding feet on the stones. And so it remains to all time a lasting record of human needs and human consolations: the voice of a brother who, ages ago, felt and suffered and renounced — in the cloister, perhaps with serge gown and tonsured head, with much chanting and long fasts, and with a fashion of speech different from ours — but under the same silent far-off heavens, and with the same passionate desires, the same strivings, the same failures, the same weariness.

— George Eliot (Marian Evans, 1820-1881), *The Mill on the Floss*

Thomas à Kempis whose book worked miracles.

Praise From Some Men of Letters

It is lawful for the solitary wight to express the love he feels for those companions so stedfast and unpresuming, that go or come without reluctance, and that, when his fellow-animals are proud, or stupid, or peevish, are ever ready to cheer the languor of his soul, and gild the barrenness of life with the treasures of bygone times.

If a Book come from the heart, it will contrive to reach other hearts; all art and author-craft are of small account to that . . . In Books lies the soul of the whole Past Time; the articulate audible voice of the Past, when the body and material substance of it has altogether vanished like a dream . . . All that Mankind has done, thought, gained, or been; it is lying as in magic preservation in the pages of Books.

— Thomas Carlyle (1795-1881)

Yours always truly
T. Carlyle

In the highest civilization the book is still the highest delight. He who has once known its satisfactions is provided with a resource against calamity. Angels they are to us of entertainment, sympathy, and provocation. With them many of us spend the most of our life — these silent guides, these tractable prophets, historians, and singers, whose embalmed life is the highest feat of art; who now cast their moonlight illumination over solitude, weariness, and fallen fortunes . . . Consider what you have in the smallest chosen library. A company of the wisest and wittiest men picked out of all civil countries, in a thousand years, have set in best order the results of their learning and wisdom . . . I hold that we have never reached the best use of books until our own thought rises to such a pitch that we cannot afford to read much. I own this loftiness is rare, and we must long be thankful to our silent friends before the day comes when we can honestly dismiss them.

— Ralph Waldo Emerson (1803-1882)

Reading is to the mind what exercise is to the body.
— Sir Richard Steele (1672-1729)

Books wind into the heart. . . . We read them when young, we remember them when old. We read there of what has happened to others; we feel that it has happened to ourselves. We owe everything to their authors, on this side barbarism . . . Even here, on Salisbury Plain, with a few old authors, I can manage to get through the summer or winter months, without ever knowing what it is to feel ennui. They sit with me at breakfast; they walk out with me before dinner — and at night, by the blazing hearth, discourse the silent hours away.

Books let us into the souls of men, and lay open to us the secrets of our own. They are the first and last, the most home-felt, the most heart-felt of all our enjoyments.

— William Hazlitt (1778-1830)

I must confess that I dedicate no inconsiderable portion of my time to other people's thoughts. I dream away my life in others' speculations. I love to lose myself in other men's minds. When I am not walking, I am reading; I cannot sit and think. Books think for me. I have no repugnances. I can read anything which I call a book. There are things in that shape, however, which I cannot allow for such. With these exceptions, I can read almost anything. I bless my stars for a taste so catholic, so unexcluding.

— Charles Lamb (1775-1834)

To divert myself from a troublesome fancy, 'tis but to run to my books. They always receive me with the same kindness. The sick man is not to be lamented, who has his cure in his sleeve. In the experience and practice of this sentence, which is a very true one, all the benefit I reap from books consists. For it is not to be imagined to what degree I please myself, and rest content in this consideration, that I have them by me, to divert myself with them when I am so disposed, and to call to mind what an ease and assistance they are to my life. 'Tis the best *viaticum* (travelling money) I have yet found out for this human journey, and I very much lament those men of understanding who are unprovided of it.

— Michel de Montaigne (1533-1592)

To divert at any time a troublesome fancy, run to thy books; they presently fix thee to them, and drive the other out of thy thoughts. They always receive thee with the same kindness.
— Thomas Fuller (1608-1661)

Faithful Companions to the End

History records instance after instance of the consolation dying men have received from the perusal of books, and many a one has made his end holding in his hands a particularly beloved volume. How dreadful must be the last moments of that person who has steadfastly refused to share the companionship and acknowledge the saving grace of books!

Numa Pompilius, the legendary second king of Rome, provided that his books should share his tomb with him. Twenty-four of these precious volumes were consigned with him to the grave. When Gabriel Rossetti's wife died, the poet cast into her open grave the unfinished volume of his poems, that being the last and most precious tribute he could pay to her cherished memory.

Plato was found dead with the *Mimes* of Sophron under his pillow in 348 B.C.

Petrarch found books faithful when princes and court beauties had proven false. His latter life was devoted entirely to their society. Indeed, one morning in 1374, he was found dead in his library at Arqua, seated at a table, with his elbow resting on the open page of a book.

In 1822 when Percy Bysshe Shelley's body was recovered after the fatal storm off Leghorn, in his coat pocket was found his well-beloved and inseparable book of poems by Aeschylus.

On January 30, 1649, at a time of civil strife between forces loyal to the king and those loyal to parliament, Charles I was beheaded by his foes in front of the Banqueting House in Whitehall, London. According to accounts of the time, Charles took his Bible with him for comfort as he mounted the scaffold to meet his doom.

The Bible which accompanied King Charles I to the scaffold.

Raleigh's Last Verse

The gallant but unfortunate Sir Walter Raleigh's history is replete with touching interest. The following lines, supposed to be the last he ever wrote, possess all the more interest for the fact of their being found written in his Bible, on the evening preceding his execution:

"Even such is Time, that takes on trust
Our youth, our joys, our all we have,
And pays us but with age and dust;
Who in the dark and silent grave,
When we have wandered all our ways,
Shuts up the story of our days:
But from this earth, this grave, this dust,
My God shall raise me up, I trust!"

— Frederick Saunders, *The Story of Some Famous Books*

"Rhetoric" by Joos van Wassenhove, circa 1470. (The National Gallery, London.)

Let my temptation be a book,
Which I shall purchase, hold, and keep.
— Eugene Field (1850-1895)

An Antique Book

A precious mouldering pleasure 'tis
To meet an antique book
In just the dress his century wore;
A privilege, I think,

His venerable hand to take,
And warming in our own,
A passage back, or two, to make
To times when he was young.

His quaint opinions to inspect,
His knowledge to unfold
On what concerns our mutual mind,
The literature of old:

What interested scholars most,
What competitions ran
When Plato was a certainty
And Sophocles a man,

When Sappho was a living girl,
And Beatrice wore
The gown that Dante deified.
Facts, centuries before,

He traverses familiar,
As one should come to town
And tell you all your dreams were true:
He lived where dreams were sown.

His presence is enchantment,
You beg him not to go;
His volumes shake their vellum heads
And tantalize, just so.

— Emily Dickinson (1830-1886)

The Perfect Pleasure

Now, my young friends, to whom I am addressing myself, with reference to this habit of reading, I make bold to tell you that it is your pass to the greatest, the purest, and the most perfect pleasures that God has prepared for his creatures. Other pleasures may be more ecstatic. When a young man looks into a girl's eye for love, and finds it there, nothing may afford him greater joy for the moment; when a father sees a son return after a long absence, it may be a great pleasure for the moment; but the habit of reading is the only enjoyment I know, in which there is no alloy. It lasts when all other pleasures fade. It will be there to support you when all other recreations are gone. It will be present to you when the energies of your body have fallen away from you. It will last you until your death. It will make your hours pleasant to you as long as you live. But, my friends, you cannot acquire that habit in your age. You cannot acquire it in middle age; you must do it now, when you are young. You must learn to read and to like reading now, or you cannot do so when you are old.

— Anthony Trollope (1815-1882)

"The Sisters" by Ralph Peacock, 1900.
(The Tate Gallery, London.)

Breathing Books

When do I love you most, sweet books of mine?
In strenuous morns when o'er your leaves I pore,
Austerely bent to win austerest lore,
Forgetting how the dewy meadows shine;
Or afternoons when honeysuckles twine
About the seat, and to some dreamy shore
Of old Romance, where lovers evermore
Keep blissful hours, I follow at your sign?

Yea! ye are precious then, but most to me
Ere lamplight dawneth, when low croons the fire
To whispering twilight in my little room,
And eyes read not, but sitting silently
I feel your great hearts throbbing deep in quire,
And hear you breathing round me in the gloom.

— Richard Le Gallienne, in *Book-Song*

What is even a wise book but a blast from the lungs made visible to the eyes?
— Hervey Allen (1889-1949)

Tread Softly

Tread softly here, as ye would tread
In presence of the honoured dead,
With reverent step and low-bowed head.

Speak low, as low as ye would speak
Before some saint of grandeur meek
Whose favour ye would humbly seek.

Within these walls the very air
Seems weighted with a fragrance rare,
Like incense burned at evening prayer.

Here may we sit and converse hold
With those whose names in ages old
Were in the book of fame enrolled.

Here under poet's power intense
We leave the world of sound and sense,
Where mortals strive with problems dense,

And mount to realms where fancy, free,
Above our poor humanity,
Roams in a joyous ecstasy.

Of if through history's maze we tread,
The hero, patriot, long since dead,
Whose great heart for his country bled,

Seems once again to work and fight
In superstition's darkest night
For God, his fellows, and the right.

Enough! mere words can never tell
The influence of the grateful spell
Which seems among these books to dwell.

— Anonymous, in *Book-Song*

An illuminated letter "B" from an Italian Psalter done in Verona, 1502. (The Victoria & Albert Museum, London.)

CHAPTER SEVEN

Bibliotypes

Some characters from the world of books
including bibliomaniacs, book hunters, bibliognosts,
eccentric authors, bibliophiles, literary lunatics,
bibliotaphs, book collectors, bibliophobes,
constant readers, bibliolaters, book borrowers,
bibliokleptomaniacs, and other bookish people.

He who has books is happy; he who does not need any is happier.
— Chinese Proverb

Some Bibliotypes

- *Bibliobibuli*— those who read too much
- *Bibliocharylodis*— a dangerous whirlpool of books likely to drown unwary readers
- *Biblioclast*— one who tears pages from books
- *Bibliodemon*— a book-fiend or demon
- *Bibliognoste*— one knowing in title pages, colophons, editions, dates and place printed, printers and all the *minutiae* of books
- *Bibliographe*— a describer of books and other literary arrangements
- *Bibliolater*— a worshipper of books
- *Biblioklept*— one who occasionally steals a book
- *Bibliokleptomaniac*— an inveterate book thief
- *Bibliolestes*— a book-robber or plunderer
- *Biblioloigos*— a book pest or plague
- *Bibliomane*— an indiscriminate accumulator of books
- *Bibliomaniac*— a book lover gone mad
- *Bibliophage*— one who eats or devours books
- *Bibliophile*— a lover of books
- *Bibliophobe*— one who fears books
- *Bibliophthor*— a book-destroyer, ravager or waster
- *Bibliotaphe*— one who buries books or hides them
- *Biblioriptos*— one who throws books around
- *Bibliosopher*— one who gains wisdom from books

A Symptom of Insanity

My poor nephew, Lord ____, was deranged. The first symptom that appeared was, his sending a chaldron of coals as a present to the Prince of Wales, on learning that he was loaded with debts. He delighted in what he called book-hunting. This notable diversion consisted in taking a volume of a book, and hiding it in some secret part of the library, among volumes of similar binding and size. When he had forgot where the game lay, he hunted till he found it.

— Horace Walpole (1717-1797)

"The Bibliomaniac" from The Ship of Fools, *1509.*

An Early Bibliomaniac

I am the first fole of all the hole navy
To kepe the pompe, the helme, and eke the sayle:
For this is my mynde, this one pleasoure have I —
Of bokes to haue great plenty and aparayle.
I take no wysdome by them: nor yet avayle
Nor them perceyve nat: And then I them despyse.
Thus am I a foole, and all that scrue that guyse.

— Sebastian Brant, *Shyp of Folys of the Worlde* (1509)

Book-Madness

In 1842 Thomas Frognall Dibdin, D.D., published *Bibliomania or Book-Madness* in which he treated Bibliomania

as a disease, the symptoms of which were a passion for:

1. Large Paper Copies . . .
2. Uncut Copies . . .
3. Illustrated Copies . . .
4. Unique Copies . . .
5. Vellum Copies . . .
6. First Editions . . .
7. True Editions . . .
8. Black Letter Editions . . .

Dr. Dibdin's prescription for curing Book-Madness included:

1. Reading useful works . . .
2. Reprints of scarce and valuable works . . .
3. Editing our best ancient Writers . . .
4. Erecting of Public Institutions . . .
5. Encouragement of Bibliography . . .

Bibliomania

A bibliomaniac must be carefully distinguished from a bibliophile. The latter has not yet freed himself from the idea that books are meant to be read. The bibliomaniac has other uses for books: he carries them about with him as talismans, he passes his time in the contemplation of their bindings, illustrations, and title pages. Some say he even prostrates himself before them in silent adoration in that joss-house which he calls his library. Bibliomaniacs are not all alike. There are numerous subdivisions. Some care only for uncut copies, some only for books printed in black letter or in italics, some for first editions, some for curious or famous bindings, while some make collections on special subjects. But all agree in this, — that the intrinsic merit of the book is a secondary consideration in comparison with its market value and exceptional scarcity.

When I get a little money, I buy books: and if any is left, I buy food and clothes.
— Desiderius Erasmus (1465-1536)

There is a story of a wealthy English collector who long believed that a certain rare book in his possession was a unique. One day he received a bitter blow. He learned that there was another copy in Paris. But he soon rallied, and, crossing over the Channel, he made his way to the rival's home. "You have such and such a book in your library?" he asked, plunging at once *in medias res.* "Yes." "Well, I want to buy it." "But, my dear sir——" "I will give you a thousand francs for it." "But it isn't for sale; I——" "Two thousand!" "On my word, I don't care to dispose of it." "Ten thousand!" and so on, till at last twenty-five thousand francs was offered, and the Parisian gentleman finally consented to part with his treasure. The Englishman counted out twenty-five thousand franc bills, examined the purchase carefully, smiled with satisfaction, and cast the book into the fire. "Are you crazy?" cried the Parisian, stooping over to rescue it. "Nay," said the Englishman, detaining his arm, "I am quite in my right mind. I, too, possess a copy of that book. I deemed it a unique. I was mistaken. Now, however, thanks to your courtesy, I know it is a unique."

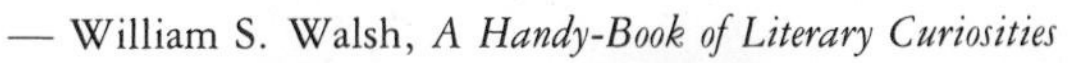
— William S. Walsh, *A Handy-Book of Literary Curiosities*

A Bookworm at work. (The Bettmann Archive, New York.)

In literature, as in love, we are astonished at what is chosen by others.
— Andre Maurois (1885-1967)

The Bookworm

With spectacles upon his nose,
He shuffles up and down;
Of antique fashion are his clothes,
His napless hat is brown.
A mighty watch, of silver wrought,
Keeps time in sun or rain,
To the dull ticking of the thought
Within his dusty brain.

To see him at the bookstall stand,
And bargain for the prize,
With the odd sixpence in his hand,
And greed in his gray eyes!
Then conquering, grasp the book, half blind,
And take the homeward track,
For fear the man should change his mind,
And want the bargain back!

The waves of life about him beat,
He scarcely lifts his gaze;
He hears within the crowded street,
The wash of ancient days.
If ever his short-sighted eyes
Look forward, he can see
Vistas of dusty libraries
Prolonged eternally.

But think not as he walks along
His brain is dead and cold;
His soul is thinking in the tongue
Which Plato spake of old!
And while some grinning cabman sees
His quaint shape with a jeer,
He smiles — for Aristophanes
Is joking in his ear.

Around him stretch Athenian walks,
And strange shapes under trees;
He pauses in a dream, and talks
Great speech with Socrates.
Then, as the fancy fails, still meshed
In thoughts that go and come,
Feels in his pouch, and is refreshed,
At touch of some old tome.

The mighty world of human kind
Is as a shadow dim,
He walks thro' life like one half blind,
And all looks dark to him;
But put his nose to leaves antique,
And hold before his sight
Some pressed and withered flowers of G
And all is life and light.

A blessing on his hair so gray,
And coat of dingy brown!
May bargains bless him every day,
As he goes up and down;
Long may the bookstall-keeper's face,
In dull times, smile again,
To see him round with shuffling pace
The corner of the lane!

A good old rag-picker is he,
Who, following, morn and eve,
The quick feet of Humanity,
Searches the dust they leave.
He pokes the dust, he sifts with care,
He searches close and deep;
Proud to discover, here and there,
A treasure in the heap.

— Robert Buchanan, *The Comic Poets*

A Lady's Rivals

Nay, seems it not most wondrous queer
That he should love to tarry here;
Prefer this "den" to boudoir nest
Where downy pillows coax to rest,
Chaise-longe and Turkish cigarette?
A stranger compound ne'er was met
Than this same creature man, I ween.
What's this dull calf to velvet sheen?
Who dares assert that this pert minx
On yellow pages in dingy inks
Is half so fair as I am, see!
What woman would not angry be
With man who turns from living charms
To worship some dead beauty's arms?
Why should he care of smiles to read
When mine so sweet are his indeed?
What's Maintenon or this L'Enclos
Or Gwynn to him, I'd like to know?
What stupid fad, what silly rage
To love such trash of bygone age!
Why, as I live, these letters mean
Just fifteen hundred seventeen.
Nay, 'tis a shame to buy such stuff
When nice new books are cheap enough;
Knew I how soon I'd be forgot
I ne'er had wedded him, God wot.
Vile, musty books, in dead skins bound —
Faugh, what an odour lingers round!
'Tis shameful taste, indeed it is:

Americans like fat books and thin women.
— Russell Baker

But hear my vow, ye loves of his,
In spite of all your dingy looks —
Apologies for decent books —
I'll win him back, ye mildewed crew,
I'll make him think I love you too!

— Anonymous, in *Book-Song*

A Literary Proposal

We stood in the bookstore together,
She chatting of this and of that;
My heart kept time with the feather
That clung to her Gainsborough hat.

On Stevenson, Stockton and Kipling,
And poets galore she enthused;
But how to propose to her, rippling
With music and laughter, I mused.

On this one and that one she tarried
To label their place on the shelf;
This "How to be Happy, Though Married":
"Absurd!" and I thought so myself.
"But those who have tried it may surely
Be trusted to know," I replied.
"I tell you," she said, "it is purely
The tone of the age to deride."

"The task for solution," I ventured,
"Is how to be married, though poor" —
I know that I ought to be censured,
She looking so sweet and demure.
Her voice was so low, 'twas the border
Of thought where it breaks into word:
"We might," she said, "solve this, in order
To prove that the book is absurd."

— Charles Knowles Bolton, in *Book-Song*

From the moment I picked up your book until I laid it down I was convulsed with laughter. Someday I intend reading it.
— Groucho Marx (1890-1977)

Some Lesser Known Authors and Their Exploits

ANDREWS, Miles Peter. Author of *Kinkvervankotfdarfpraken-gotchderns,* a farce imitated from Lady Craven; *Dissipation,* a comedy, and *Reparation,* a comedy; each of which have taken their station in the regions of mediocrity.

COTTON, Charles, M.D. The proprietor of a private madhouse near St. Albans, and author of *Visions in Verse for the Instruction of Younger Minds.*

EON, Madame. This very extraordinary woman lived more than twenty years in a public station in the disguise and under the character of a man. She was secretary to the French Embassy at London, of the Count de Guerchy, and was instrumental in negotiating the peace of Paris in 1763. Her *Letters, Memoirs and Negociations* were published in quarto in the year 1764. Her sex at length became a topic for public suspicion, and the speculation of gamesters, and was authentically ascertained in a trial before Lord Mansfield founded upon one of these speculations. . . . She is much celebrated for her skill in fencing, tennis, and other manly exercises.

HURD, Richard, D.D. Bishop of Worcester, and Clerk of the Closet to the King. . . . The distinguishing feature of the mind of Bishop Hurd seemed to be intellectual cowardice.

INGLEFIELD, John, a captain in the navy. He published a pamphlet intitled *Narrative of the Loss of the Centaur;* and there have been about half-a-dozen pieces of the same dimensions published in a controversy of some notoriety between him and his wife.

O'KEEFE, John, a native of Ireland, and late a performer upon the Dublin Theatre. He owes his genius as a poet to the accident of having demolished his wife's nose in a fit of jealousy. . . . His style is chiefly that of pun, and the happy production of voluble nonsense. . . . Mr. O'Keefe has the misfortune of being deprived of the use of his organs of sight.

SCOTT, Martha, a poetess. Author of a performance entitled *The Female Advocate,* which has had between two and three admirers.

TASKER, William, a clergyman, and a writer of poetry. He commenced his career about the year 1779; and produced an *Ode to the Warlike Genius of Great Britain;* an *Ode to the Memory of the Bishop of Sodor and Man.* . . . Mr. Tasker's writings are not good prose, because they are tagged with rhymes; and they are not good poetry, because they are cold, insipid, pleonastic, and prosaical.

TRIMMER, Delphine, a devout lady who has dedicated her slender talents to the instructing from the press the rising generation. Her works are, *Sacred History* in four volumes duodecimo; and a little *Spelling Book.*

TYTLER, Alexander, a professor of universal history in the University of Edinburgh. He published in 1783 a *Syllabus of his Lectures on Universal History;* and in 1784 was the first person in these islands who adventured in an air balloon, though for want of being able to afford the expense, he only sailed over two barns and a stable.

— *Catalogue of Five Hundred Celebrated Authors of Great Britain Now Living* (1788)

All poets are mad.
— Robert Burton (1577-1640)

A riotous book reading drawn by William Hogarth, 1775.

It is the glory and merit of some men to write well, and of others not to write at all.
— Jean De La Bruyère (1646-1696)

Jeremy Bentham lived here with his cane, teapot, and cat.

An Author at Home

Jeremy Bentham was an English philosopher who wrote in his various books that the end of life is happiness and that the highest morality is the pursuit of the greatest happiness by the greatest number. He lived in London (in a house once owned by John Milton) where he steadfastly refused to see visitors for the last fifty years of his life.

Like Franklin in appearance, he made a curious picture; his white hair, long and flowing, his neck bare; in a quaker-cut coat, list shoes, and white worsted stockings drawn over his breeches' knees. In his garden, in this odd guise, he might be seen trotting along on what he called his "ante-prandial circumgyrations." Indoors, he dined in his workroom, where the green window curtains were pinned over with slips of paper, being notes taken at the moment of passing thoughts, to be located and collated at a future time. Until he died on June 4, 1832, Bentham lived alone with his walking stick, named Dapple, his teapot, named Dickey, and his cat, named the Reverend Doctor John Langborne.

An Author of U.S. Independence Is Bathed

In 1776, I was present, at Providence, Rhode Island, in a social assembly of most of the prominent leaders of the state. I recollect that the subject of independence was cautiously introduced by an ardent Whig, and the thought seemed to excite the abhorrence of the whole circle. A few weeks after, Thomas Paine's *Common Sense* appeared, and passed through the continent like an electric spark. It everywhere flashed conviction, and aroused a determined spirit, which resulted in the Declaration of Independence upon the 4th of July ensuing. The name of Paine had resounded throughout Europe. I often officiated as interpreter,although humbled and mortified at his filthy appearance, and awkward and unseemly address. As he had been roasted alive on his arrival at L'Orient, and well basted with brimstone, he was absolutely offensive and perfumed the whole apartment. He was soon rid of his respectable visitors, who left the room with marks of astonishment and disgust. I took the liberty, on his asking for a loan of a clean shirt, of speaking to him frankly of his dirty appearance and brimstone odour, and prevailed upon him to stew for an hour in a hot bath. This, however, was not done without much entreaty, and I did not succeed until, receiving a file of English newspapers, I promised, after he was in the bath, he should have the reading of them, and not before. He at once consented, and accompanied me to the bath, where I instructed the keeper in French (which Paine did not understand) to gradually increase the heat of the water, until "le Monsieur était bien bouilli." He became so absorbed in his reading that he was nearly parboiled before leaving the bath, much to his improvement and my satisfaction.

— Elkanah Watson, *Men and Times of the Revolution* (1856)

Stanley's Shrinking Library

(During his quest for Dr. Livingstone, Stanley's reading material diminished progressively.)

You ask me what books I carried with me to take across Africa. I carried a great many — three loads, or about 180 lbs. weight; but as my men lessened in numbers stricken by famine, fighting, and sickness, they were one by one reluctantly thrown away, until finally, when less than 300 miles from the Atlantic, I possessed only the Bible, Shakespeare, Carlyle's *Sartor Resartus,* Norie's *Navigation,* and *Nautical Almanac* for 1877. Poor Shakespeare was afterwards burned by demand of the foolish people of Zinga. At Bonea, Carlyle, and Norie, and *Nautical Almanac* were pitched away, and I had only the old Bible left.

— H.M. Stanley, *Pall Mall Gazette*

A Complete Literary Character

Isaac Disraeli, author of *Curiosities of Literature,* devoted his life to books. His son, Benjamin, who became prime minister of England, describes his father:

"He was himself a complete literary character, a man who really passed his life in his library. Even marriage produced no change in these habits; he rose to enter the chamber where he lived alone with his books, and at night his lamp was ever lit within the same walls. Nothing, indeed, was more remarkable than the isolation of this prolonged existence; and it could only be accounted for by the united influences of three causes: his birth, which brought him no relations or family acquaintance; the bent of his disposition; and the circumstance of his inheriting an independent fortune, which rendered unnecessary those exertions that would have broken up his self-reliance. He disliked business, and he never required relaxation; he was absorbed in his pursuits. In London his only amusement was to ramble among booksellers; if he entered a club, it was only to go into the library. In the country, he scarcely ever left his room but to saunter in abstraction upon a terrace; muse over a chapter, or coin a sentence."

— Benjamin Disraeli (1804-1881)

Isaac Disraeli lived and breathed books.

Where is human nature so weak as in the bookstore?
— Henry Ward Beecher (1813-1887)

Buying a Book from Ben Franklin

One fine morning when Franklin was busy preparing his newspaper for the press, a lounger stepped into the store, and spent an hour or more looking over the books, etc., and finally taking one in his hand, asked the shop-boy the price.
"One dollar," was the answer.
"One dollar," said the lounger, "can't you take less than that?"
"No, indeed; one dollar is the price."
Another hour had nearly passed, when the lounger said —
"Is Mr. Franklin at home?"
"Yes, he is in the printing-office."
"I want to see him," said the lounger.
The shop-boy immediately informed Mr. Franklin that a gentleman was in the store, waiting to see him. Franklin was soon behind the counter, when the lounger, with book in hand, addressed him thus:
"Mr. Franklin, what is the lowest you can take for that book?"
"One dollar and a quarter," was the ready answer.
"One dollar and a quarter! Why, your young man asked me only a dollar."
"True," said Franklin, "and I could have better afforded to have taken a dollar then, than to have been taken out of the office."
The lounger seemed surprised, and wishing to end the parley of his own making, said —
"Come, Mr. Franklin, tell me what is the lowest you can take for it?"
"One dollar and a half."
"A dollar and a half! Why, you offered it yourself for a dollar and a quarter."
"Yes," said Franklin, "and I had better have taken that price then, than a dollar and a half now."
The lounger paid down the price, and went about his business — if he had any — and Franklin returned into the printing-office.

— William Keddie, *Anecdotes Literary and Scientific*

This will never be a civilized country until we expend more money for books than we do for chewing gum.
— Elbert Hubbard (1859-1915)

American Book Habits

In 1978, a study inquiring into the nature of reading and book buying habits of the American public revealed that 54 percent of the men and 46 percent of the women do not read books. Of those who do read, women outnumber men 58 percent to 42 percent and buy more books, 59 percent to 41 percent.

The reasons given by the non-readers include: "Don't like to read, don't have time, poor eyesight, not interested, don't read well, work is more important, prefer television, prefer other leisure activities" and "reading puts me to sleep".

Those who read books do so for general knowledge (76 percent), for pleasure (74 percent), to relax (51 percent), for career information (39 percent), as a time-filler (21 percent), for religious or spiritual reasons (22 percent), as an escape (23 percent), for educational purposes (24 percent).

47 percent of Americans read their books at night before going to sleep, while 39 percent read in the evening after dinner. Three percent read while commuting to work and 6 percent during their lunch hour.

The favorite reading places are the living room and in bed (47 percent each), with libraries and bathrooms equally popular (6 percent).

— Source: *Book Industry Study Group Report No. 6* prepared by Yankelovich, Skelly and White, Inc., 1978

British Bookshop Behavior

A survey conducted in 1980 revealed something of the behavior of the book buyer in British bookshops. 3,000 people were interviewed twice at 51 bookshops, first as they entered the shop and again as they left.

More than 50 percent of the people had no intention of buying a book at all but were presumably intent on browsing, getting a free read or seeking shelter from the rain. Of those intent on a purchase, 25 percent had a specific title in mind, 25 percent were looking for a book on a particular subject, and 30 percent were going to buy a book as a gift.

Only 33 percent of the interviewees bought a book and 45 percent of these were impulse purchases. The major reason given for the non-purchases was "the information chaos in the head of the customer". One of the 3,000 people interviewed at the entrance of a bookshop failed to reappear again. He was found asleep in the basement two hours later.

— Source: *Lost Book Sales* by TBL Book Services Ltd.

Biblio*kleptomania*

The world, as I know from my books, is full of abominable evil; even some of these books have never been returned.
— Logan Pearsall Smith (1865-1946)

is a modern euphemism which softens the ugly word book-thief by shrouding it in the mystery of the Greek language.

The roll of book-thieves, if it included all those who have prigged without detection or who have borrowed without returning, would doubtless include the most illustrious men of all ages. It will include learned men, wise men, good men, — the highest dignitaries of church and state, even a pope. And that pope was no less a man than Innocent X. To be sure, he was not pope, but plain Monsignor Pamphilio, when he stole a book from Du Moustier, the painter, — his one detected crime. But who shall say it was his only crime? To be sure, again, Du Moustier was something of a thief himself: he used to brag how he had prigged a book of which he had long been in search from a stall on the Pont-Neuf. Nevertheless, he strenuously objected to be stolen from. When, therefore, Monsignor Pamphilio, in the train of Cardinal Barberini, paid a visit to the painter's studio in Paris and quietly slipped into his soutane a copy of "L'Histoire du Concile de Trente," M. Du Moustier, catching him in the act, furiously told the cardinal that a holy man should not bring thieves and robbers in his train. With these and other words of a like libellous nature he recovered the "History of the Council of Trent", and kicked out the future pontiff. Historians date from this incident that hatred to the crown and the people of France which distinguished the pontifical reign of Innocent X.

Among royal personages, the Ptolemies were book-thieves on a large scale. An entire department in the Alexandrian Library, significantly called "Books from the Ships," consisted of rare volumes taken from sea-voyagers who touched at the port. True, the Ptolemies had a conscience. They were careful to have fair transcripts made of these valuable manuscripts, which they presented to the visitors; but, as Aristotle says, and, indeed, as is evident enough to minds of far inferior compass, the exchange, being involuntary, could not readily be differentiated from robbery. Brantôme tells us that Catherine de Médicis, when Marshall Strozzi died, seized upon his very valuable library, promising some day to pay the value to his son, but the promise was never kept.

Perhaps the greatest of biblioklepts was Don Vincente, a friar of that Poblat convent whose library was plundered and dispersed at the pillage of the monasteries during the regency of Queen Christina in 1834. Coming to Barcelona, he established himself in a gloomy den in the book-selling quarter of the town. Here he set up as a dealer, but fell so in love with his accumulated purchases that only want tempted him to sell them. Once at an auction he was outbid for a copy of the "Ordinacions per los Gloriosos Reys de Arago," — a great rarity, perhaps a unique. Three days later the house of the successful rival was burned to the ground, and his blackened body, pipe in hand, was found in the ruins. He had set the house on fire with his pipe — that was the general verdict. A mysterious succession of murders followed. One bibliophile after another was found in the streets or the river, with a dagger in his heart. The shop of Don Vincente was searched. The "Ordinacions" was discovered. How had it escaped the flames that had burned down the purchaser's house? Then the Don confessed not only that murder but others. Most of his victims were customers who had purchased from him books he could not bear to part with. At the trial, counsel for the defence tried to discredit the confession, and when it was objected that the "Ordinacions" was a unique copy, they proved there was another in the Louvre, that, therefore, there might be still more, and that the defendant's might have been honestly procured. At this, Don Vincente, hitherto callous and silent, uttered a low cry. "Aha!" said the alcade, "you are beginning to realize the enormity of your offence!" "Yes," sobbed the penitent thief, "the copy was not a unique, after all."

— William S. Walsh, *A Handy-Book of Literary Curiosities*

Bibliokleptomaniacs at work.

Never lend books, for no one ever returns them: the only books I have in my library are books that other folk have lent me.
— Anatole France (1844-1924)

A Circulating Library

How hard, when those who do not wish
To lend, that's lose, their books,
Are snared by anglers — folks that fish
With literary hooks;

Who call and take some favorite tome,
But never read it through,
They thus complete their set at home,
By making one at you.

Behold the bookshelf of a dunce
Who borrows — never lends:
Yon work, in twenty volumes, once
Belonged to twenty friends.

New tales and novels you may shut
From view — 'tis all in vain;
They're gone — and though the leaves are 'cut'
They never "come again."

For pamphlets lent I look around,
For tracts my tears are spilt;
But when they take a book that's bound,
'Tis surely extra-gilt.

A circulating library
Is mine — my birds are flown
There's an odd volume left to be
Like all the rest, alone . . .

— Laman Blanchard, *Poetical Works* (1876)

BOOK KEEPING TAUGHT IN ONE LESSON
"DONT LEND THEM"

Welcome Home Borrowed Book

I really am obliged to you for bringing back my book,
It moves me much to look whereon I thought no more to look;
It 'minds me of the early time when it was lent to you,
When life was young and hope was fair, and this old book was new.

How well does memory recall the gilt that on it shone
The day I saw it, coveted, and bought it for my own;
And vividly I recollect you called around that day,
Admired it, then borrowed it, and carried it away!

And now it comes to me again across the lapse of time,
Wearing the somewhat battered look of those beyond their prime.
Old book, you need a rest — but ere you're laid upon the shelf,
Just try and hang together till I read you through myself.

— Anonymous, in *Book-Song*

Books and Thieves

A good book steals the mind from vain pretences,
From wicked cogitations and offences,
It makes us know the world's deceiving pleasures,
And set our hearts on never-ending treasures.

Men know not thieves from true men by their looks,
Nor by their outsides, no man can know books:
Both are to be suspected, all can tell,
And wise men ere they trust will try them well.
A book may be a title good and fair,
Though in it one may find small goodness there.

— John Taylor, *An Arrant Thief* (1625)

A Warning

Steal not this book, my worthy friend,
For fear the gallows will be your end;
Up the ladder, and down the rope,
There you'll hang until you choke;
Then I'll come along and say —
"Where's that book you stole away?"

— A favorite inscription in old school books

EX-LIBRIS
MCM
S

CHAPTER EIGHT

Ex Libris

How to choose from the far too many books available (avoiding the bad, dull, lewd, smutty, and worthless), when, where, and how to read them, and advice on their care and handling.

An incurable itch for scribbling takes possession of many, and grows inveterate in their insane breasts.
— Juvenal (60-140)

Too Many Books

When wise Koheleth long ago —
Though when and how the pundits wrangle —
Complained of books, and how they grow
And twist poor mankind's brain a-tangle,
He did not dream the fatal fangle
To such a pitch would e'er extend,
And such a world of paper mangle —
Of making books there is no end.

The poets weep for last year's snow,
About the porch the schoolmen dangle,
The owl-like eyes of science glow
O'er arc, hypothenuse, and angle;
The playwrights mouth, the preachers jangle,
The critics challenge and defend,
And Fiction turns the Muses' mangle —
Of making books there is no end.

Where'er we turn, where'er we go,
The books increase, the bookmen brangle:
Our bookshelves groan with row on row
Of nonsense typed in neat quadrangle.
Better to burn the lot and twangle
An honest banjo; better tend
To ride and box and shoot and angle —
Of making books there is no end.

Envoy:
Few books are worth a copper spangle:
Come forth, and choose, my dusty friend,
The ranchman's rope, the nautch-girl's bangle —
Of making books there is no end.

— Justin Huntley McCarthy, in *Book-Song*

On the Multiplicity of Bad Books

It is the case with literature as with life; wherever we turn we come upon the incorrigible mob of humankind, whose name is Legion, swarming everywhere, damaging everything, as flies in summer. Hence the multiplicity of bad books, those exuberant weeds of literature which choke the true corn. Such books rob the public of time, money, and attention, which ought properly to belong to good literature and noble aims, and they are written with a view merely to make money or occupation. They are therefore not merely useless, but injurious. Nine-tenths of our current literature has no other end but to inveigle a thaler or two out of the public pocket, for which purpose author, publisher, and printer are leagued together. A more pernicious, subtler, and bolder piece of trickery is that by which penny-a-liners and scribblers succeed in destroying good taste and real culture. Hence the paramount importance of acquiring the art *not* to read; in other words, of not reading such books as occupy the public mind, or even those which make a noise in the world, and reach several editions in their first and last year of existence. We would recollect that he who writes for fools finds an enormous audience, and we should devote the ever scant leisure of our circumscribed existence to the master-spirits of all ages and nations, those who tower over humanity, and whom the voice of Fame proclaims: only such writers cultivate and instruct us. Of bad books we can never read too little: of the good never too much. The bad are intellectual poison and undermine the understanding. Because people insist on reading not the best books written for all time, but the newest contemporary literature, writers of the day remain in the narrow circle of the same perpetually revolving ideas, and the age continues to wallow in its own mire.

— Arthur Schopenhauer (1788-1860), *Parerga und Paralipomena*

Bad Books

Bad books through eyes and ears do break and enter,
And take possession of the heart's frail centre,
Infecting all the little kingdom man
With all the poisonous mischief that they can,
Till they have robbed and ransacked him of all
Those things which men may justly goodness call.

— J. Taylor, *An Arrant Thief* (1874)

Of making many books there is no end; and much study is a weariness of the flesh.

— Ecclesiastes, The Bible

Bloterature Versus Literature

(From the statutes of St. Paul's School in London written by its founder, John Colet (1467-1519).)

"The books shall be Erasmus's *Copia, Lactantius, Prudentius, Juvencus, Proba* and *Sedulius,* and *Baptista Mantuanus,* and such other as shall be thought convenient and most to purpose unto the true Latin speech; all barbary, all corruption, all Latin adulterate, which ignorant blind fools brought into this world, and with the same hath distained and poisoned the old Latin speech, and the veray Roman tongue, which, in the time of Tully, and Sallust, and Virgil, and Terence, was used — I say, that filthiness, and all such abusion, which the later blind world brought in, which more rather may be called BLOTERATURE than LITERATURE, I utterly banish and exclude out of this School."

— quoted by Thomas Frognall Dibdin in *Bibliomania*

I couldn't write the things they publish now, with no beginning and no end, and a little incest in the middle.
— Irvin S. Cobb (1876-1944)

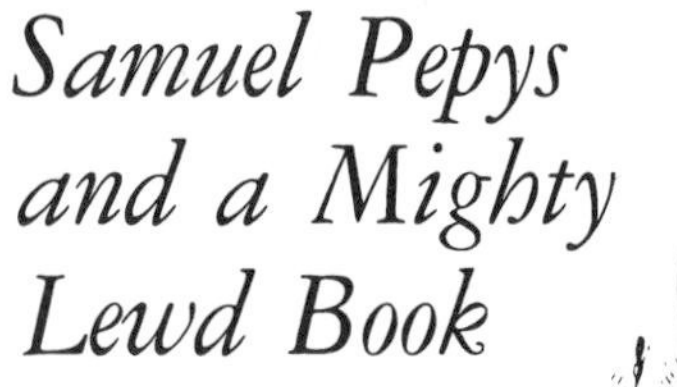

Samuel Pepys and a Mighty Lewd Book

January 13th, 1668:
"Thence homeward by coach and stopped at Martin's, my bookseller, where I saw the French book which I did think to have had for my wife to translate, called *L'escholle des Filles,* but when I come to look in it, it is the most bawdy, lewd book that ever I saw, so that I was ashamed of reading in it, and so away home."

February 8th:
"Thence away to the Strand to my bookseller's, and there staid an hour, and bought the idle, rogueish book *L'escholle des Filles,* which I have bought in plain binding, avoiding the buying of it better bound, because I resolve, as soon as I have read it, to burn it, that it may not stand in my list of books, nor among them, to disgrace them if it should be found."

February 9th:
"Doing business, and also reading a little of *L'escholle des Filles,* which is a mighty lewd book, but yet not amiss for a sober man once to read over to inform himself in the villainy of the world."

(That evening):
"I read through *L'escholle des Filles,* a lewd book, but what do no wrong once to read for information sake . . . And after I had done it I burned it that it might not be among my books to my shame, and so at night to supper and to bed."

— Samuel Pepys, *Diary*

(*L'escholle des Filles,* by Helot, was publicly burnt along with its author in effigy, in 1672)

"The Reading Girl" by Theodore Roussel. (The Tate Gallery, London.)

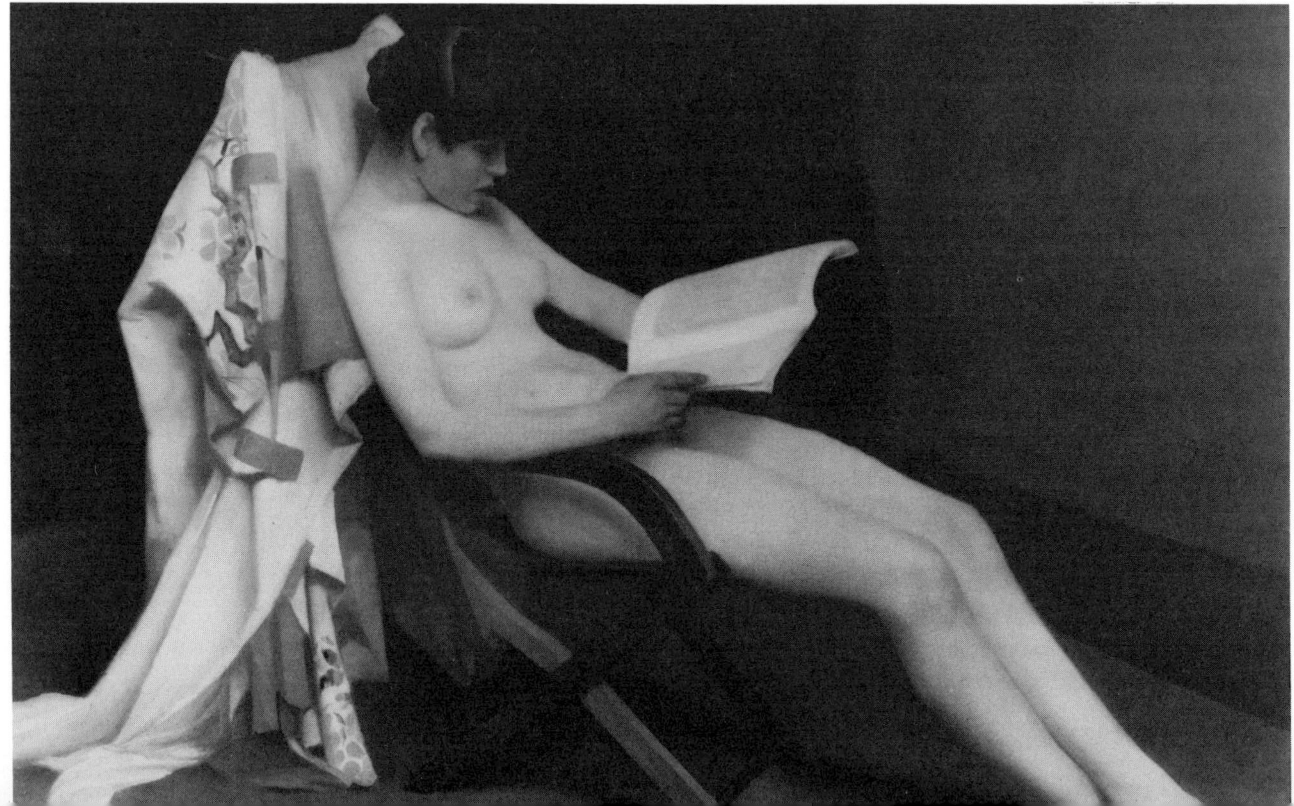

Trashy American Literature

The character of the American literature is, generally speaking, pretty justly appreciated in Europe. The immense exhalation of periodical trash, which penetrates into every cot and corner of the country, and which is greedily sucked in by all ranks, is unquestionably one great cause of its inferiority.

Another obvious cause of inferiority in the national literature, is the very slight acquaintance with the best models of composition, which is thought necessary for persons called well educated.

— Frances Trollope (1780-1863), *Domestic Manners of the Americans*

Satanic English Literature

This great English people among so many good and solid qualities has one vice which spoils these very qualities. From Shakespeare to Milton, from Milton to Byron, their beautiful and sombre literature is sceptical, judaic, satanic, to sum up anti-Christian.

— Jules Michelet (1798-1874), *L'Histoire de France*

The bookplate of Aubrey Beardsley (1872–1897), one of the great book illustrators.

It is the sexless novel that should be distinguished: the sex novel is now normal.

— George Bernard Shaw (1856-1950)

The Smell (and Bad Breath) of Books

We have it upon the authority of William Blades that books breathe; however, the testimony of experts is not needed upon this point, for if anybody be sceptical, all he has to do to convince himself is to open a door of a bookcase at any time and his olfactories will be greeted by an outrush of odors that will prove to him beyond all doubt that books do actually consume air and exhale perfumes.

Visitors to the British Museum complain not unfrequently that they are overcome by the closeness of the atmosphere in that place, and what is known as the British Museum headache has come to be recognized by the medical profession in London as a specific ailment due to the absence of oxygen in the atmosphere, which condition is caused by the multitude of books, each one of which, by that breathing process peculiar to books, consumes several thousand cubic feet of air every twenty-four hours.

Professor Huxley wondered for a long time why the atmosphere of the British Museum should be poisonous while other libraries were free from the poison; a series of experiments convinced him that the presence of poison in the atmosphere was due to the number of profane books in the Museum. He recommended that these poison-engendering volumes be treated once every six months with a bath of cedria, which is a solution of the juices of the cedar tree; this, he said, would purge the mischievous volumes temporarily of their evil propensities and abilities.

— Eugene Field, *The Love Affairs of a Bibliomaniac*

If one cannot enjoy reading a book over and over again, there is no use in reading it at all.
— Oscar Wilde (1854-1900)

How to Recognize a Bad Book

We find in the greater number ot works, leaving out the very bad, that their authors have thought, not seen — written from reflection, not intuition. And this is why books are so uniformly mediocre and wearisome. For what an author has thought, the reader can think for himself; but when his thought is based on intuition, it is as if he takes us into a land we have not ourselves visited. All is fresh and new. . . . We discover the quality of a writer's thinking powers after reading a few pages. Before learning what he thinks, we see how he thinks — namely, the texture of his thoughts; and this remains the same, no matter the subject in hand. The style is the stamp of individual intellect, as language is the stamp of race. We throw away a book when we find ourselves in a darker mental region than the one we have just quitted. Only those writers profit us whose understanding is quicker, more lucid than our own, by whose brain we indeed think for a time, who quicken our thoughts, and lead us whither alone we could not find our way.

— Arthur Schopenhauer (1788–1860), *Parerga und Paralipomena*

You Can't Tell a Book by Its Cover

On my study shelves they stand,
Well known all to eye and hand
Bound in gorgeous cloth of gold,
In morocco rich and old,
Some in paper, plain and cheap,
Some in muslin, calf, and sheep;
Volumes great and volumes small
Ranged along my study wall.
But their contents are past finding
By their size or by the binding.

There is one with gold agleam,
Like the Sangreal in a dream,
Back and boards in every part
Triumph of the binder's art;
Costing more, 'tis well believed,
Than the author e'er received.
But its contents? Idle tales,
Flappings of a shallop's sails!
In the treasury of learning
Scarcely worth a penny's turning.

Here's a tome in paper plain,
Soiled and torn and marred with stain,
Cowering from each statelier book
In the darkest, dustiest nook.
Take it down, and lo! each page
Breathes the wisdom of a sage!
Weighed a thousand times in gold,
Half its worth would not be told,
For all the truth of ancient story
Crowns each line with deathless glory.

On my study shelves they stand;
But my study walls expand,
As mind's pinions are unfurled,
Till they compass all the world.
Endless files go marching by,
Men of lowly rank and high,
Some in broadcloth, gem-adorned,
Some in homespun, fortune-scorned;
But God's scales that all are weighed in
Heed not what each man's arrayed in.

— Willis Fletcher Johnson, in *Book-Song*

My Library

Then shall my library be devote
To the magic of Niddy-Noddy,
Including the volumes which Nobody wrote
And the works of Everybody.

— Eugene Field, *Love Affairs of a Bibliomaniac*

In 1977 Americans bought more than 300,000 copies of* The Nothing Book*, cloth bound and containing 192 blank pages.

The Fashionable Craze for Books

What is the use of books and libraries innumerable, if scarce in a lifetime the master reads the titles? A student is burdened by a crowd of authors, not instructed; and it is far better to devote yourself to a few, than to lose your way among a multitude.

Thousands of books were burnt at Alexandria. I leave others to praise this splendid monument of royal opulence, as for example Livy, who regards it as "a noble work of royal taste and royal thoughtfulness." It was not taste, it was not thoughtfulness, it was learned extravagance — nay not even learned, for they had bought their books for the sake of show, not for the sake of learning — just as with many who are ignorant even of the lowest branches of learning, books are not instruments of study, but ornaments of dining-rooms. Procure then as many books as will suffice for use; but not a single one for show.

You will find then in the libraries of the most arrant idlers all that orators or historians have written — bookcases built up as high as the ceiling. Nowadays a library takes rank with a bathroom as a necessary ornament of a house. I could forgive such ideas, if they were due to extravagant desire for learning. As it is, these productions of men whose genius we revere, paid for at a high price, with their portraits ranged in line above them, are got together to adorn and beautify a wall.

— Lucius Annaeus Seneca (4 B.C.-65 A.D.)

Never read anything until not to have read it has bothered you for some time.
— Samuel Butler (1612-1680)

A Common Sewer for Rubbish

Desultory reading is indeed very mischievous, by fostering habits of loose, discontinuous thought, by turning the memory into a common sewer for rubbish of all thoughts to float through, and by relaxing the power of attention, which of all our faculties most needs care, and is most improved by it. But a well-regulated course of study will no more weaken the mind than hard exercise will weaken the body; nor will a strong understanding be weighed down by its knowledge, any more than oak is by its leaves, or than Samson was by his locks. He whose sinews are drained by his hair, must already be a weakling.

Above all, in the present age of light reading, that is of reading hastily, thoughtlessly, indiscriminately, unfruitfully, when most books are forgotten as soon as they are finished, and very many sooner, it is well if something heavier is cast now and then into the midst of the literary public. This may scare and repel the weak, it will rouse and attract the stronger, and increase their strength, by making them exert it. In the sweat of the brow, is the mind as well as the body to eat its bread.

— Julius C. Hare (1795-1855)

The Vice of Reading

Reading is a stumbling block, a cloak thrown over ignorance, a softening, demoralising, relaxing practice, which, if persisted in, will end by enfeebling the minds of men and women, making flabby the fibre of their bodies, and undermining the vigour of nations.

The habit of novel reading, novel upon novel for reading's sake, is the principal cause of the general vice of reading; novel-drinking is not so expensive, so outwardly repulsive, as dram-drinking, nor can it be said that it brings the

"A world of disorderly notions, picked out of his books, crowded his imagination." — Don Quixote as seen by Gustave Doré.

same ruin and disgrace upon families — but the individual is as surely enfeebled by it, taste corrupted, will unstrung, understanding saddened.

— Anonymous, *The Vice of Reading* (1874)

Authors Usually Dress for a Visit

In conversing with books we may choose our company, and disengage without ceremony or exception. Here we are free from the formalities of custom and respect: we need not undergo the penance of a dull story, from a fop of figure; but may shake off the haughty, the impertinent, and the vain, at pleasure. Besides, authors, like women, commonly dress when they make a visit. Respect to themselves makes them polish their thoughts, and exert the force of their understanding more than they would, or can do, in ordinary conversation: so that the reader has as it were the spirit and essence in a narrow compass, which was drawn off from a much larger proportion of time, labour, and expense.

— Jeremy Collier (1647-1705), *Essays Upon Several Moral Subjects*

Types of Readers

Readers may be divided into four classes:

1. Sponges, who absorb all they read and return it nearly in the same state, only a little dirtied.
2. Sand-glasses, who retain nothing and are content to get through a book for the sake of getting through the time.
3. Strain-bags, who retain merely the dregs of what they read.
4. Mogul diamonds, equally rare and valuable, who profit by what they read, and enable others to profit by it also.

— Samuel Taylor Coleridge (1772-1834)

A Formula for Reading the History of the World

(Based on reading for six hours every day)

For a knowledge of Sacred History	3 months
Ancient Egypt, Babylon, and Assyria	1 month
Greek History	6 months
Roman History by the moderns	7 months
Roman History by the original writers	6 months
Ecclesiastical History, general & particular	30 months
Modern History	24 months
To this may be added for recurrences & re-perusals	48 months
	Total 125 months
	or 10 years 5 months

— Lenglet du Fresnoy, a French scholar of the eighteenth century

A learned fool is one who has read everything and remembered it.

— Josh Billings (1818-1885)

The Art of Skipping

Almost every author is a sort of half-caste printer, and understands thoroughly, that, in order to have a book make a respectable exterior appearance, there must be a certain number of pages, and each chapter, for the sake of general appearance and combined effect, must be of a certain length. In order to comply with this printers' requirement, the author resorts to what is known in printers' parlance as "padding." Whether there be ideas or not, and whether the author has anything worth saying or not, makes not a whit of difference. The chapters must be of uniform length. So there is appended to a little wheezy engine of a thought a long train of words that weary the eye to count. Every idea is hammered and elaborated with instance after instance, until it is so thin that it breaks on inspection. Almost any sort of trumpery by way of allusion is lugged in by the ears, and the longest words in the most incomprehensible sentences are introduced. The same sort of patchwork and piecing is practiced in dramatic representations. When there is a "stage-wait" for any reason, a street-scene is pushed on in the first grooves, and two actors are sent on to hold a conversation on any subject they choose, for the amusement of the audience, and to keep up the interest while the trouble is being repaired behind the scenes. This is what is known in histrionic dialect as "gagging," —a species of trickery practiced in all professions, and not unknown to the noble brotherhood of authors. The best thing that can be done with it is to do nothing with it. Skip it.

— J.C. Van Dyke, *Books and How to Use Them*

A man may as well expect to grow stronger by always eating as wiser by always reading.
— Jeremy Collier (1650-1726)

The Rules of Reading

The best rule of reading will be a method from nature, and not a mechanical one of hours and pages. It holds each student to a pursuit of his native aim, instead of a desultory miscellany. Let him read what is proper to him, and not waste his memory on a crowd of mediocrities. The three practical rules which I have to offer are:

1. Never read any book that is not a year old.
2. Never read any but famed books.
3. Never read any but what you like; or in Shakespeare's phrase,
   "No profit goes where is no pleasure ta'en;
   In brief, sir, study what you most affect."

— Ralph Waldo Emerson (1803-1882)

Food for Thought

❦ As long as the aliments of which we have partaken retain their own nature and float as solids in our stomach, they are burdensome; but when they have changed from their former state, then, and not till then, they enter into our strength and blood. Let us do the same with the foods which nourish our minds, so that we do not suffer the things we have taken in to remain whole and foreign. Let us digest them! otherwise they enter our memory, but not our mind.

— Seneca (4 B.C.-65 A.D.)

❦ We ought to regard books as we do sweetmeats, not wholly to aim at the pleasantest, but chiefly to respect the wholesomest; not forbidding either, but approving the latter most.

— Plutarch (46-120)

❦ Reading is free, and does not exhaust itself with the act, but may be repeated, in case you are in doubt, or wish to impress it deeply on the memory. Let us repeat it; and — just as we swallow our food masticated and nearly fluid, in order that it may be more easily digested — so our reading should not be delivered to the memory in its crude state, but sweetened and worked up by frequent repetition.

— Quintilian (42-115)

❦ If all thy pipes of wine were fill'd with books,
Made of the barks of trees, or mysteries writ
In old moth-eaten vellum, he would sip thy cellar
Quite dry, and still be thirsty. Then, for's diet,
He eats and digests more volumes at a meal,
Than there would be larks (though the sky should fall)
Devour'd in a month in Paris.

— John Fletcher (1576-1625)

❦ Read not to contradict and confute, nor to believe and take for granted, nor to find talk and discourse, but to weigh and consider. Some books are to be tasted, others to be swallowed, and some few to be chewed and digested; that is, some books are to be read only in parts; others to be read, but not curiously; and some few to be read wholly, and with diligence and attention.

— Francis Bacon (1561-1626)

A Private Literary Teapot

Society is a strong solution of books. It draws the virtue out of what is best worth reading, as hot water draws the strength of tea leaves. If I were a prince, I would hire or buy a private literary teapot, in which I would steep all the leaves of new books that promised well. The infusion would do for me without the vegetable fibre. You understand me; I would have a person whose sole business should be to read day and night, and talk to me whenever I wanted him to.

— Oliver Wendell Holmes (1809-1894)

Bookmarks With Legs and Handles

Professor A. De Morgan points out the great utility of book-markers, and tells us how they may be best made. A rectangular slip of paper is doubled into two, and then one half is again doubled. One half of the whole slip then forms the marker, the other half a pair of legs, to hold it in its place, bestriding the top of the leaf. He recommends a thin paper to make the marker of. He recommends also another marker useful for unbound sheets, which we give in his own words:

> "Let the rectangular slip be doubled sideways, so as to present a marker and what we may call a handle joined at a bevelled crease. The handle should then be inserted between the leaves at the back, the marker acting as usual. It is next to impossible to keep the common marker in its place among loose leaves. This second kind of marker will be better than the common one even for bound books, the handle being made short and thrown well into the back of the leaf."

— *Notes and Queries* (1868)

Tea and Buttered Muffin Bookmarks

Charles Lamb's (1775-1834) ideas of book-marking are to be found in his correspondence with Coleridge. "A book reads the better," he writes, "which is our own, and has been so long known to us that we know the topography of its blots and dog's-ears, and can trace the dirt in it to having read it at tea with buttered muffins, or over a pipe, which I think is the maximum."

Whenever Edward Young (1683-1765), the poet, came to a striking passage in his reading he folded the leaf, and at his death books were found in his library which had long resisted the power of closing.

When Montaigne (1553-1592) got to the end of a volume which he considered unworthy to be re-read, it was his custom to jot down in it the time he had read it, as well as his considerations as to its worth.

Voltaire's (1694-1778) practice was to note in the books he read, whatever of censure or approbation they deserved. A friend of his used to complain that the works he lent him were returned always *disfigured* by his remarks.

When interrupted in his studies, John Selden (1584-1654) put his spectacles into the book as a marker, and there often forgot them. When his valuable library, which he bequeathed to the University of Oxford, came to be examined, these curious markers were found by the dozens.

— J.R. Rees, *The Diversions of a Book-Worm*

As sheer casual reading-matter, I still find the English dictionary the most interesting book in our language.
— Albert Jay Nock (1873–1945)

Reading by means of the Elater Noctilicus (Firefly).

A book is a mirror: if an ass peers into it, you can't expect an apostle to peer out.
— Georg Christoph Lichtenberg (1742-1799)

Of Showing Honorable Respect in the Care of Books

First, then, let there be considerate moderation in the opening and shutting of books, that they be not opened in headlong haste nor, when our inspection is ended, be thrown away without being duly closed. For we ought to care far more diligently for a book than for a boot. But the race of scholars is commonly educated badly and, unless it be curbed by the rules of its elders, becomes accustomed to endless childishness. They are moved by petulance; they swell with presumptuousness; they give judgment as though certain of everything, whereas they are expert in nothing.

You shall chance to see some stiff-necked youth sluggishly seating himself for study, and while the frost is sharp in the winter time, his nose, all watery with the biting cold, begins to drip. Nor does he deign to wipe it with his cloth until he has wet the books spread out before him with the vile dew. Would that such a one were given in place of a book a cobbler's apron! He has a nail almost as black as jet and reeking with foul filth, and with this he marks the place of any matter that pleaseth him. He sorts out innumerable straws which he sets in divers places, evidently that the mark may bring back to him what his memory cannot hold. These straws, because the stomach of the book does not digest them and no one takes them out, at first distend it beyond its wonted place of closing and at length, being quite overlooked, begin to rot. He halts not at eating fruits and cheese over the open page and, in a slovenly way, shifts his cup hither and thither. And because he has not his alms bag at hand, he casts the residue of the fragments into the book. With endless chattering he ceases not to rail against his companions and, while adducing a multitude of reasons void of all sensible meaning, wets the books spread out in his lap with the sputtering of his spittle. And what shall I say more? Soon doubling his elbows, he reclines upon the book and by his short study invites a long sleep and, by spreading out the wrinkles, bends the margins of the leaves, doing no small harm to the volume.

And now the rain is over and gone, and the flowers have appeared on the earth. Then the scholar whom we are describing, a neglecter rather than an inspector of books, will stuff his book with the violet, the primrose and the rose, yea, also with the quatrefoil. Then he will apply his watery hands, all damp with sweat, to turning over the volumes. Then will he pound on the white parchment with his dusty gloves, and line by line hunt over the page with a fusty leather finger. Then, at the nip of the biting flea the holy book is flung aside, and scarcely being shut within a month's time, becomes so swollen with the dust that has fallen in it that it cannot obey the effort of one who would close it.

Especially, moreover, must we restrain impudent youths from handling books — those youths who, when they have learned to draw the shapes of letters, soon begin, if opportunity be granted them, to be uncouth scribblers on the best volumes and, where they see some larger margin about the text, make a show with monstrous letters; and if any other triviality whatsoever occurs to their imagination, their unchastened pen hastens at once to draw it out. There the Latinist and the sophister and every unlearned scribe proves the goodness of his pen, a practice which we have seen to be too often injurious to the best of books, both as concerns their usefulness and their price.

There are also certain thieves who make terrible havoc by cutting off the margins for paper on which to write their letters, leaving only the written text; or they turn to various abuses the flyleaves which are bound in for the protection of the book. This sort of sacrilege ought to be prohibited under pain of anathema.

It greatly suits with the honorable behavior of scholars that so often as they return to their study after eating, a washing should always precede their reading. Nor should a finger smeared with grease turn over the leaves or loosen the clasps of the book. Let no crying child admire the pictures in the capital letters, lest he defile the parchment with his wet hand, for he touches instantly whatever he sees. Laymen, moreover, who look in the same way at a book

The best effect of any book is that it excites the reader to self-activity.
— Thomas Carlyle (1795-1881)

lying upside down as when it is open in its natural way, are wholly unworthy the intercourse of books. Let the clerk see to this also, that no dirty scullion greasy from his pots and yet unwashed shall touch the lilies of the books; but he that walketh without blemish shall minister to the precious volumes. Again, a becoming cleanness of hands would add much both to books and scholars, if it were not that the itch and pimples are marks of the clergy. As often as defects of books are noticed, we must quickly run to mend them; for nothing lengthens faster than a slit, and a rent which is neglected at the time will be repaired afterward with usury.

Moses, the meekest of men, instructs us in the thirty-first chapter of Deuteronomy how to make in a becoming way bookshelves for books, where they may be kept safe from all injury. "Take," saith he, "this book and put it in the side of the ark of the covenant of the Lord your God." Oh, fitting place and seemly library! made of imperishable shittim wood and overlaid round about with gold without and within! But all unfitting neglect in handling books is excluded by the example of our Savior Himself, as we read in the fourth chapter of Luke. For when He had read the prophetic scripture concerning Himself in the book that was handed Him, He did not give back the book to the minister until He had closed it with His own most sacred hands. By this, students are taught most clearly that not even that which is least in the care of books should be neglected.

— Richard de Bury, *The Philobiblon* (1345)

An eighteenth century reading aid.

Often I sat up in my room reading the greatest part of the night, when the book was borrowed in the evening and to be returned early in the morning, lest it should be missed or wanted.

— Benjamin Franklin (1706-1790)

A nineteenth century device for reading in bed.

Recipes for the Care and Cleaning of Books

To Kill and Prevent Bookworms.

Take 1 ounce of camphor, powdered like salt, 1 ounce of bitter apple, cut in halves, mix, and spread on the bookshelves, and renew every eight or ten months. (N.B. If bitter apple (Colocynth) cannot be procured, use tobacco.)

To Remove Stains of Oil, Grease, etc.

Chlorine water, or a weak solution of chloride of lime, removes stains, and bleaches the paper at the same time, but this involves pulling the book to pieces. If the stains are small, they may be removed with a weak solution of chloride of lime — a piece, the size of a nut, to a pint of water, a camel's hair pencil, and plenty of patience.

Polishing Old Bindings.

Take the yolk of an egg, beat it up with a fork, apply it with a sponge, having first cleansed the leather with a dry flannel. When the leather is broken, rubbed, or decayed, rub a little paste into the parts to fill up the holes, otherwise the glair would sink into them and turn them black. To produce a polished surface a hot iron must be passed over the leather.

Perfume of Books.

Musk, with one or two drops of oil of Neroli, sponged on each side of the leaves and hung up to dry, will give a powerful odor. A more simple plan is, to place a vial of the mixture on the bookcase, or place there pieces of cotton impregnated with oil of cedar or of birch.

— John Power, *A Handy-Book about Books*

How to Hold it . . .

When the religious are engaged in reading in cloister or in church, they shall if possible hold the books in their left hands, wrapped in the sleeve of their tunics, and resting on their knees; their right hands shall be uncovered with which to hold and turn the leaves of the aforesaid books. (a rule of the Benedictine monks in the middle ages)

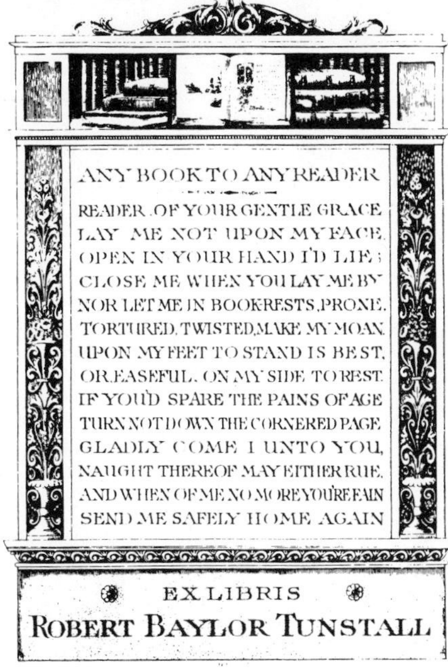

The Reason Why . . .

I beseech you, my friend, when you are reading my book to keep your hands behind its back, for fear you should do mischief to the text by some sudden movement; for a man who knows nothing about writing thinks that it is no concern of his. Whereas to a writer the last line is as sweet as port is to a sailor. Three fingers hold the pen, but the whole body toils. Thanks be to God. I Warembert wrote this book in God's name. Thanks be to God. Amen. (found in a book in a French monastery, circa 1523)

Or Else . . .

This book belongs to S. Maximin at his monastery of Micy, which abbat Peter caused to be written, and with his own labour corrected and punctuated, and on Holy Thursday dedicated to God and S. Maximin on the altar of St. Stephen, with this imprecation that he who should take it away from thence by what device soever, with the intention of not restoring it, should incur damnation with the traitor Judas, with Annas, Caiaphas, and Pilate. Amen. (from a Benedictine monastery in France)

Amen . . .

Should anyone by craft or any device whatever abstract this book from this place may his soul suffer, in retribution for what he has done, and may his name be erased from the book of the living and not be recorded among the Blessed. (from the sixteenth century Missal of Robert at Jumièges, France)

This book is John Smith's,
My fist is another;
You touch one
And you'll feel the other.

— John Smith, from his schoolbook

The Laws of Books

Nor shall a man write any accounts upon the pages of a book or scribble anything on any part of it.

One must be careful not to keep his books in the same receptacle with food, for fear of the mice nibbling them both.

If one is unable to press the leaves of a book together in order to fasten the clasp, he shall not place his knees upon it to force it to close.

If a father dies, and leaves a dog and a book to his sons, one of the children shall not say to the other, "You take the dog and I'll have the book," for what a disgraceful contrast are these two objects!

If one wishes to take a nap, he must first cover his books up, and not recline upon them.

If a book has fallen to the ground, and at the same time some money or a sumptuous garment has fallen also, he shall first pick up the book. If a fire breaks out in his house, he shall first rescue his books, and then his other property. Nor shall he ever think the time spent upon attending to books wasted; and even if he finds a book so full of errors as that correction of them would be useless, he shall not destroy the book, but place it in some out-of-the-way corner.

A man is obliged to be very careful as to the respect due to books, for by not acting thus he is behaving offensively to his fellow-man, whose brain has produced these books.

— Rabbi Judahben Samuel Sir Leon Chassid, *Sefer Chassidon* (Book of the Pious), Regensburg, Germany (1190)

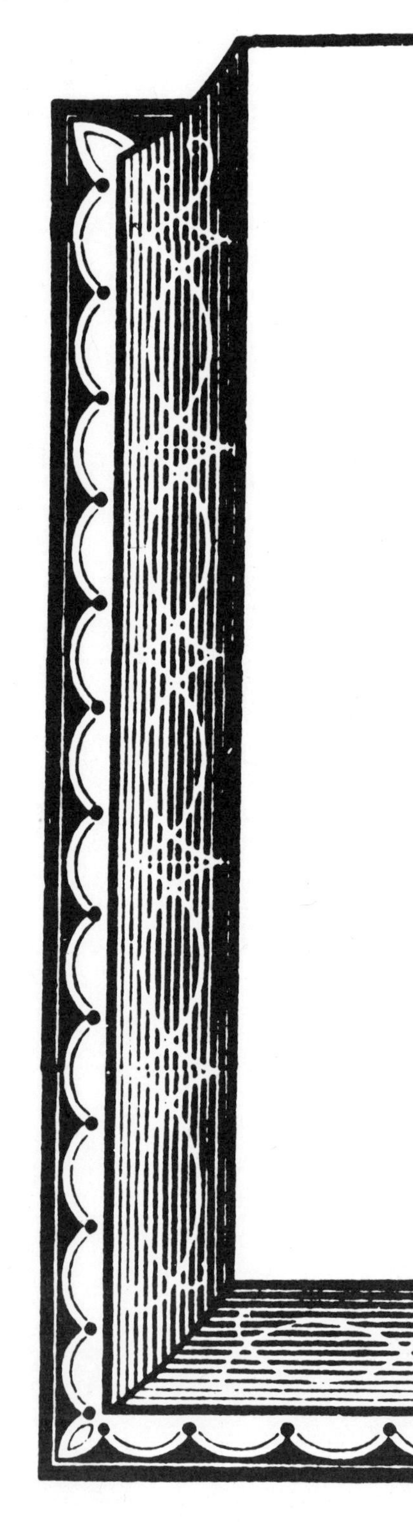

Go Little Book

Go, little book, and wish to all
Flowers in the garden, meat in the hall,
A bin of wine, a spice of wit,
A house with lawns enclosing it,
A living river by the door,
A nightingale in the sycamore!

— Robert Louis Stevenson (1850-1894)

END OF THE VOLUME.

There are more books upon books than upon all other subjects.
— Michel de Montaigne (1533-1592)

Bibliography

Adams, W. Davenport. *The Comic Poets.* London: George Routledge and Sons, 1876.

Allen, Charles Dexter. *American Book-Plates.* New York: Macmillan and Co., 1894.

Andrews, William. *Literary Byways.* London: William Andrews & Co., 1898.

Barr, James. *American Humorous Verse.* London: Walter Scott, 1891.

Beresford, James. *Bibliosophia, or Book Wisdom.* London: 1810.

Blades, William. *Books in Chains.* London: Elliot Stock, 1892.

______. *The Enemies of Books.* London: Elliot Stock, 1902.

______. *The Pentanteuch of Printing.* Chicago: A.C. McClury and Company, 1891.

Blumenthal, Walter Hart. *Bookmen's Bedlam.* Freeport, New York: Books for Libraries Press, 1955.

Books and Bookmen.

The Bookseller.

The Bookworm.

Bouchot, Henri. *The Book.* London: H. Grevel & Co., 1890.

Brewer, Luther. *The Love of Books.* Cedar Rapids, Iowa: L. and E. Brewer, 1923.

Broadus, Edmund Kemper. *Books and Ideals.* London: Oxford University Press, 1921.

Browne, Irving. *In Track of the Bookworm.* 1897.

Buchner, Rudolph. *Bucher und Menschen.* Berlin: Bertelsmann GmbH, 1976.

Burton, John Hill. *The Book Hunter.* Edinburgh: William Blackwood & Sons, 1900.

Chambers, Robert. *The Book of Days.* London & Edinburgh: W. & R. Chambers, Ltd., 1865.

Clark, John Willis. *The Care of Books.* Cambridge: The University Press, 1901.

Clouston, William Alexander. *Literary Curiosities and Eccentricities.* London: Ward, Lock & Tyler, 1875.

Combe, William. *The Tour of Dr. Syntax.* London: 1812.

Crane, Walter. *Of the Decorative Illustration of Books Old and New.* London: B. Bell & Sons Limited, 1921.

Davenport, Cyril. *By-Ways among English Books.* London: Methuen, 1927

De Bury, Richard. *The Philobiblon.* Berkeley and Los Angeles, California: Copyright 1948 by the Regents of the University of California Press; excerpts reprinted by permission of the University of California Press.

Derome, Lucien. *Le Luxe des Livres.* Paris: 1879.

Dibdin, Thomas Frognall. *The Bibliomania.* London: Henry G. Bohn, 1842.

Dill, Francis Parsons. *The Ideal Book.* 1932.

Disraeli, Isaac. *The Calamaties and Quarrels of Authors.* London: Routledge, Warne, and Routledge, 1893.

______. *Curiosities of Literature.* London: Edward Moxon, 1838.

Ditchfield, Peter Hampson. *Books Fatal to Their Authors.* London: Elliot Stock, 1895.

Donaldson, Elizabeth and Gerald. *The Book of Days.* New York: A&W Publishers, Inc., 1979.

Downs, Robert. *Famous Books, Ancient and Medieval.* New York: Barnes & Noble, 1964.

Egan, M.F. *Confessions of a Book Lover.* 1922.

Farrer, James Anson. *Books Condemned to Be Burnt.* London: Elliot Stock, 1892.

______. *Literary Forgeries.* London: Longmans, Green, 1907.

Febvre, Lucien. *The Coming of the Book.* London: N.L.B., 1976.

Ferriar, John. *The Bibliomania.* London: T. Cadell, and W. Davies, 1809.

Field, Eugene. *The Love Affairs of a Bibliomaniac.* London: John Lane, 1896.

Fielding, Henry. *Author's Farce.* 1730.

Fitch, George Hamlin. *Comfort Found in Good Old Books.* San Francisco: Paul Elder and Company, 1911.

Gale Research Company. *The Story of the Bookplate.* Detroit: Gale Research Company, 1971.

Haight, Anne Lyon. *Banned Books.* New York: R.R. Bowker, 1978.

Hanks, Henry. *A California Bookworm.* San Francisco: Microscopical Society, 1897.

Harrison, Frederick. *A Book about Books.* London: John Murray, 1943.

Hooke, Robert. *Micrographia.* London: 1665.

Ireland, Alexander. *The Booklover's Enchiridion.* London: Simpkin, Marshall & Co., 1888.

Jackson, Holbrook. *The Anatomy of Bibliomania.* New York: Farrar, Straus, 1950.

______. *The Fear of Books.* London: The Soncino Press, 1932.

Jackson, W. Spencer. *Merry Minstrelsy.* London: Howe & Co., 1892.

Johnson, Fridolph. *A Treasury of Bookplates.* New York: Dover Publications, Inc., 1977.

Johnson, F. and Hornung, C.P. *200 Years of American Graphic Art.* New York: George Brazillier, 1976.

Keddie, William. *Anecdotes Literary and Scientific.* London: James Blackwood & Co., 1894.

Lang, Andrew. *Books and Bookmen.* London and New York: Longmans, Green, & Co., 1892.

Levarie, Norma. *The Art and History of Books.* New York: James H. Heineman, 1968.

Madan, Falconer. *Books in Manuscript.* London: Kegan Paul, Trench, Trubner & Co., 1893.

Mathews, Brander. *Ballads of Books.* New York: George J. Coombes, 1887.

McMurtrie, Douglas Crawford. *The Book.* New York: Oxford University Press, 1943.

Merryweather, F. Somner. *Bibliomania in the Middle Ages.* London: Merryweather, 1869.

O'Conor, J.F.X. *Facts about Bookworms.* London: Suckling & Company, 1898.

Orcutt, William Dana. *The Kingdom of Books.* Boston: Little, Brown & Co., 1927.

Oswald, John Clyde. *A History of Printing.* New York: D. Appleton and Company, 1928.

Parke, Walter. *Patter Poems.* London: Vizetelly & Co., 1885.

Parton, J. *The Humorous Poetry of the English Language.* New York: Mason Brothers, 1860.

Pinner, H. *The World of Books in Classical Antiquity.* Leiden: A. W. Sijthoff, 1948.

Pollard, Alfred William. *Old Picture Books.* London: Methuen and Co., 1902.

———. *Early Illustrated Books.* New York: Empire State Book Company, 1926.

Power, John. *A Handy-Book about Books.* London, John Wilson, 1870.

Pritchard, Francis Henry. *Books and Readers.* London: George G. Harrap, 1931.

Publisher's Weekly.

Rees, Rogers. *The Diversions of a Bookworm.* London: Elliot Stock, 1886.

Roberts, William. *The Book-Hunter in London.* Chicago: A.C. McClurg & Co., 1895.

———. *Book-Verse.* London: Elliot Stock, 1896.

Russell, W. Clarke. *The Book of Authors.* London and New York: Frederick Warne and Co., 1890.

Saunders, Frederick. *The Story of Some Famous Books.* London: Elliot Stock, 1887.

Smith, Charles John. *Historical and Literary Curiosities.* London. Henry G. Bohn, 1847.

Smith, Edward. *Foreign Visitors in England.* London: Elliot Stock, 1889.

Starrett, Vincent. *Books Alive.* New York: Random House, 1940.

———. *Bookman's Holiday.* New York: Random House, 1942.

Targ, William. *Bouillabaisse for Bibliophiles.* Metuchen, New Jersey: Scarecrow Reprint Corporation, 1968.

TBL Book Services Ltd. *Lost Book Sales.* London: 1980.

Thomas, G. Alan. *Great Books and Book Collectors.* London: Weidenfeld and Nicolson, 1975.

Thompson, L.S. *Notes on Bibliokleptomania.* 1944.

Trithemus, Johannes. *In Praise of Scribes.* Lawrence, Kansas: Coronado Press, 1974.

UNESCO. *Statistical Year Books.* (annual)

Van Dyke, J.C. *Books and How to Use Them.* New York: Fords, Howard, and Hulbert, 1883.

Walsh, William Shepard. *A Handy-Book of Literary Curiosities.* Philadelphia: J.B. Lippincott Company, 1892.

Webber, Winslow Lewis. *Books about Books.* Boston: Hale, Cushman & Flint, 1937.

Werdet, Edmond. *Histoire du Livre.* Paris: E. Dentu, 1864.

Wheatley, B. Henry. *The Dedication of Books.* London: Elliot Stock, 1887.

———. *Literary Blunders.* London: Elliot Stock, 1893.

———. *How To Make an Index.* London: Elliot Stock, 1902.

White, Beatrice. *Philobiblon.* London: The Library Association, 1967.

White, Gleeson. *Book-Song.* London: Elliot Stock, 1893.

Wooton, Christopher B. *Trends in Size, Growth and Cost of Literature Since 1955.* London: The British Library, 1977.

Yankelovich, Skelly and White, Inc. *Reading and Book Purchasing.* New York, 1978.

Subject Index

Author Index